GOOD DIGGING

THE STORY OF ARCHAEOLOGY

by Dorothy and
Joseph Samachson

Illustrated with photographs and maps

RAND McNALLY & COMPANY
NEW YORK • CHICAGO • SAN FRANCISCO

Dedicated to

Miriam and Michael

CONTENTS

ILLUSTRATIONS

Maps of the areas discussed
appear at the heads of most chapters

INTRODUCTION:
WHAT IS ARCHAEOLOGY?

ARCHAEOLOGISTS ARE GREAT TREASURE HUNTERS. MANY OF THEIR treasures would sell for little on the market, although they are extremely valuable for what they tell us of human history, and fortunes are sometimes spent in finding them. Occasionally, discoveries have great financial as well as cultural value—the golden treasures of Troy, of Mycenae in Greece, and of Egyptian Pharaohs, for example—and then the world at large becomes as excited about them as the archaeologists. Most finds, however, are less spectacular—perhaps the eye shadow used by an Egyptian beauty, a battered amulet with which a Cretan or a Trojan kept evil spirits away, or the chipped flint arrowhead with which a primitive hunter secured his day's food.

Scientist and ditch-digger, detective and treasure hunter—the archaeologist must be all these and more. The men and women who devote themselves to the fascinating science of ancient civilizations must practise a sort of magic. From old scrolls and shattered pottery, from broken-armed statues and ruined temples, they must first reconstruct a picture of the past and then breathe life into it. They must take us traveling through time, so that we of the twentieth century A.D. may know how men and women thought and felt thousands of years ago.

Picking up a stray legend here, a baffling reference in an almost worn-out manuscript there, at times nothing more than a strange local name or superstition, archaeologists slowly fit together isolated bits of evidence of long-forgotten people and cities. Sponsored by their governments, by private research foundations, or by universities, they then organize expeditions that help uncover the final proof. Some of their greatest discoveries are thus carefully and logically planned. Others are the result of brilliant "hunches" or of blind luck, but an alert mind is also required to take advantage of the hunch or the luck.

Archaeology deals with the dead, but it is itself very much alive. It has made great contributions to medicine, astronomy, literature, painting, sculpture, and to the study of language, and has in turn received much from them. Nowadays archaeologists must know chemistry and physics, as well as other physical and biological sciences. From this you may rightfully conclude that an archaeologist needs long and thorough preparation for his work. Later we shall see how he prepares for his career, and we shall learn how from his study of the past we can better understand our present and help predict our future. But first, let us define our subject more closely. Let us learn where archaeology begins and where it ends—if it ever does.

I-THE BEGINNINGS
OF ARCHAEOLOGY

ARCHAEOLOGISTS ARE INTERESTED IN ANCIENT MAN, AND THEY seek evidence of the past in what is left of man himself, of his surroundings, and of the things he made, known as artifacts. They are concerned with these material objects, not for their value as museum pieces or works of art, but for what they tell of ancient man's life and culture.

When excavators disinter a heap of long dead bones or unwind the wrappings of a mummy, they learn how tall our ancestors were, what diseases afflicted them, whether they lost their teeth early, and so on. Some of these seemingly unimportant details give us an idea of the way the ancients lived. Perhaps an archaeologist of the future, observing the numerous cavities in the teeth of the present generation, may be able to deduce that Americans and Europeans eat too many desserts and drink too many soft drinks. From no more than a battered television set he might guess a great deal about the mid-twentieth century mode of life.

When did archaeology begin? In one sense it began with ancient man himself, from the moment he realized that before him had lived man still more ancient. King Nabonidus, the last king of Babylon, who lived some twenty-five hundred years ago, was interested in the ruins he found in his own kingdom, and made a number of excavations. But the spirit of his digging was more that of religion than of science. At Ur of the Chaldees, which readers of the Bible may recall as the home of Abraham, he rebuilt a tower-shrine that had been destroyed centuries before. He was in fact so interested in resurrecting the glories of the Babylonian past that he neglected to defend his own kingdom properly. Later historians have ascribed his defeat at the hands of the Persians at least partly to this neglect, and have used it to emphasize the dangers which result from too great an interest in archaeology.

Nabonidus was one of many rich or noble persons who, through the centuries, have been fascinated by the creations of previous ages. Most of these individuals, however, were not concerned with the cultures their relics represented. They were more collectors of antiques than archaeologists in the modern sense.

There were, however, even in the ancient world, individuals interested in the writings and other remains of what was to *them* an ancient world. The Greek historian, Herodotus, who has been described as the father of history, has been cred-

A gold fluted bowl from the Royal Cemetery at Ur (2600 B.C.)

ited with fathering anthropology and archaeology as well. Herodotus gave descriptions of the customs of non-Greek peoples who lived both before and during his own lifetime. In his *History* he recounts in fascinating detail stories about the Persians, the Babylonians, the Egyptians, and many other ancient peoples. Sometimes he was outrageously wrong, a victim of his own prejudices. But often he told of events and gave descriptions of cities which later investigators were able to confirm. To give one example: his description of the size of Babylon was long considered an absurd exaggeration until two thousand years later excavators uncovered these walls and proved that Herodotus had been telling the truth.

The title of father of archaeology has also been conferred upon Thucydides, another Greek historian, and Lucretius, a Roman poet. And Horapollon, an Egyptian who lived in the fourth century B.C., wrote a treatise on hieroglyphics, the ancient Egyptian writing, and is described in histories of science as an archaeologist.

Whether these ancient scholars actually deserved the title is to a large extent a matter of opinion, and not all archaeologists agree. They do agree that before modern archaeology could develop and emerge from its shell it needed a long period of incubation.

Archaeology approached the level of modern scholarship in the eighteenth century. It was not then a science. A science is a branch of human knowledge that consists of a complicated mixture of well-established fact and theory along with a number of much more dubious facts and of guesses which do not yet deserve to be called theory. Eighteenth-century archaeology had too few facts at its disposal, and what was worse, it did not know how to interpret them. Without a reasonably correct interpretation of facts, there is no science. As time went on, however, archaeology did become more and more dependent on facts, and there is little question that it is a science now.

The story of how it became one has a fascination all its own. It starts in Italy.

II - THE HERITAGE
OF A VOLCANO

VESUVIUS IS A VOLCANO NOT FAR FROM NAPLES ALONG THE ITALIAN coast. It has erupted at irregular intervals as far back as historical records go, and as a result its slopes as well as the surrounding countryside are carpeted with a layer of ash which has provided extremely fertile soil for vineyards. Through the centuries, peasants have cultivated the soil in the shadow of the peak itself, usually in total disregard of the danger.

In 1748, while digging an irrigation canal, a peasant struck his spade against a stone wall. Further digging brought to light the well-preserved remains of a number of completely buried houses whose very existence had been forgotten hundreds of years before. News of the discovery spread from the local authorities to art collectors and to scholars. Soon, under the auspices of the King of Naples, excavation began in earnest, and the royal museums began to fill with ancient Roman objects. Since then, for more than two centuries, digging has continued with hardly a pause for war or revolution, and the two ancient cities of Pompeii and Herculaneum are now largely uncovered.

Shortly after that first clang of spade against stone, modern archaeological scholarship began. Not that the objects recovered from Pompeii were the first known examples of ancient art. During the fifteenth century, and especially after the

A courtyard and villa in Herculaneum

fall of Constantinople to the Turks in 1453, refugee scholars brought to western Europe many beautiful works, some of them created in the most glorious days of Greece and Rome. Long before the rediscovery of Pompeii it had become fashionable to collect the treasures of the ancient world, to acquire masterpieces of weathered sculpture with which to adorn gardens and palaces, to hoard gold and ornaments which might grace the charms of a sixteenth- or seventeenth-century beauty.

It became equally profitable to supply these items to those who wanted to be in fashion. For many centuries the tombs of the great, especially of kings, had been sources of treasure. The profession of grave- and tomb-robbing was at least five thousand years old. When interest in the past was reawakened, it acquired an army of new members who pillaged burial places dating back to the times of the Romans or even before.

Unlike archaeologists, the looters kept only those articles which had market value. They took what they could sell, melting down objects that were of awkward or unpopular shape. The rest they either threw away or left behind, to be discovered generations later.

In this way much of the art of Greece and Rome was destroyed. Some, however, was preserved in the collections of the rich or noble all over Europe.

Collectors were also interested, however, in other objects of less obvious value. In many countries farmers and excavators ran across old flint tools, occasionally in the company of human bones. They were usually regarded as "thunderbolts" or "fairy arrows," although toward the end of the eighteenth century a few individuals, who were thought somewhat unbalanced, did attribute them to primitive people. But what primitive people could there have been before Adam?

As time went on, searchers discovered not only flint tools

but objects of bronze and iron. Gradually these became part of various collections. They made good subjects for conversation, and their owner rejoiced in the name of "antiquarian," but he was usually under no illusion that his assemblage of battered pieces of stone or metal was of any genuine importance. He collected not for science but for enjoyment, as most stamp collectors do now.

In a world where collecting was done in this fashion by dabblers in art or antiquarianism, the discovery of Pompeii had the impact of an electric shock. Some of the treasures uncovered at Pompeii were disappointing, consisting of objects used in everyday life, made of bronze or glass rather than gold. But enough was found of interest and value to keep enthusiasm alive.

As new objects were added to old collections, the private museums began to overflow. The wealthy men who owned them now discovered a use for a previously useless type of human being—the scholar. A man who had studied both art and antiquity might be able to arrange and classify the contents of different museums, might compare one with another, might reassure a prince that his particular collection was the most interesting and valuable in the world.

From the scholar's point of view, of course, the opportunity to compare different collections was invaluable. One such scholar, Johann Joachim Winckelmann, born in 1717, traveled all over Europe, and in 1764 published his *History of Ancient Art,* which attempted to classify the objects recovered from the ancient world. Among these objects the finds at Pompeii occupied a leading place.

Winckelmann's work stimulated the further collection of material which archaeology was later to study. This had its uses, but like many other contributions to archaeology, was a mixed blessing. Materials were dug up, but usually no records were made of the digging. Valuable objects were saved, but the "trivial" were discarded. Excavators had yet to learn that "trivial" objects might at times be the most important. Proper methods of excavation had not yet been developed, and as a result later scholars were often to belittle the work of the colleagues who came before them.

There were other students of ancient art besides Winckelmann, and it would be unjust to give him all the credit. Moreover, Winckelmann's main effort, to properly classify ancient art, was unsuccessful. For a half century after his death, although much work was done, all other efforts were equally unsuccessful. One great difficulty was the impossibility of tracing any relation between the objects of ancient Rome and those left by primitive man. So long as these latter were considered thunderbolts and fairy arrows, there was no hope.

Meanwhile, the excavations at Pompeii continued. A city put to death by a volcano offered the modern world special treasures. Fire had destroyed much, but whatever had survived and been buried in ashes had an excellent chance of preservation. And an enormous number of commonplace objects survived at Pompeii. The oil lamps, the pitchers, the broken pottery, the mosaics on the floors, and the pictures on the walls all helped to give their discoverers an insight into ancient Roman life that mere jewels or golden ornaments could not.

For a hundred years after the rediscovery of the buried city, workers dug through the most important buildings in the hope of finding objects of artistic value. Excavation was not always a mere matter of shoveling aside soft volcanic ash to uncover the stone buildings below. In addition to the ash and cinders, the original eruption had emitted streams of lava, which flowed over a wide area and later hardened into stone. And subsequent eruptions left a criss-cross of similar stone ribbons through and between the layers of ash, so that diggers could not at first know when they would run into one of these strips of hardened lava. These were not only difficult to cut through, but if the excavators were too vigorous, they might easily ruin the walls of an ancient building under the impression that they were simply getting a lava flow out of the way. Even in the early days, excavation required skilled supervision.

Gradually, as years passed, the nature of the work changed. In 1860, a new director, Giuseppe Fiorelli, began to uncover the city one area at a time, layer by layer. Fifty years later, the Italian government decided to remove the rich volcanic ash which had buried Pompeii for use as topsoil in the reclamation of swampy ground. Not only were the objects of art left where they were found, but attempts were made to restore the houses to their original condition. The skeleton of Pompeii, dug up from its grave, became a museum in which the life of the old Roman city was displayed.

What sort of life had it been? For the most part, a prosperous and comfortable one. Pompeii did a thriving business in wine and grain, but it was a residential resort as well, the home of many well-to-do Romans. Its twenty thousand inhabitants had their choice of two theatres, an amphitheatre for gladiatorial games, capable of seating the entire population at once, two large athletic fields, a swimming pool, and three public baths. It had a fine Forum, which was an open-air place of assembly, as well as numerous temples for the worship of Jupiter, Apollo, Venus, Isis, and other gods. The temples, with their statues of the different divinities, added beauty to what was already a handsome city.

There was another feature of the landscape that might be said to have added a touch of beauty—the slopes of Vesuvius, visible not far in the background. Vesuvius had obviously erupted in the past, for Pompeii was built on lava, and its streets were paved and its buildings constructed of this same

The Civil Forum of Pompeii, Vesuvius in the background

useful stone. But for centuries the volcano had remained on its best behavior, so that the danger of new eruptions had been forgotten.

In the year 63 A.D. the Pompeiians were given a stern reminder. A powerful earthquake convulsed the entire area and destroyed many buildings. Soon after the ground had become quiet again, the Pompeiians began to rebuild. But many sections of the city were still waiting for repairs in August of 79 A.D. And by then it was too late.

New quakes had shaken the ground and created turbulent waves on the surface of the nearby sea. The volcano suddenly came alive, spouting smoke and flame. Yet the inhabitants of Pompeii and the nearby towns, frightened as they were, hesitated to flee. There was no living memory of what past eruptions had done. And hadn't many of the buildings of Pompeii and nearby Herculaneum survived the first earthquake? It seemed more sensible to remain at home and ride out the danger indoors than to risk the open countryside.

On August 24th the volcano put an end to such thoughts. Smoke and ashes exploded into the air, blackening the sky, and only flashes of lightning from the hot, electrically charged dust illuminated the doomed cities. The stench of poisonous gases filled the air, while bubbling lava poured down the slopes of Vesuvius.

Some finally sought and found safety in flight. But of those who hid in cellars or underground rooms, not one escaped. In the barracks of the gladiators near the theatre, archaeologists later dug up sixty-three skeletons. Two thousand people died in Pompeii alone, most of them poisoned by gases emitted by the volcano. Centuries later, excavators were able to reconstruct the scene of devastation. Tapping the ground, they located hollow regions which they filled with plaster and allowed to harden. Then, stripping away the mass of volcanic ash, they beheld plaster casts of the unfortunate victims—men, women, even a chained dog—as tragic and as revealing of despair as if made at the very moment of death.

Some of the Pompeiians who had escaped waited until the fiery graveyard which was left of their home town had cooled slightly and returned to salvage what was undestroyed, including marble slabs that could be used in new buildings. But the city as a whole was beyond salvaging. Most of the survivors moved to a nearby city and began life anew. Pompeii and Herculaneum became no more than names in a few books by ancient writers—until that fateful day when the spade of a peasant brought them back to mind.

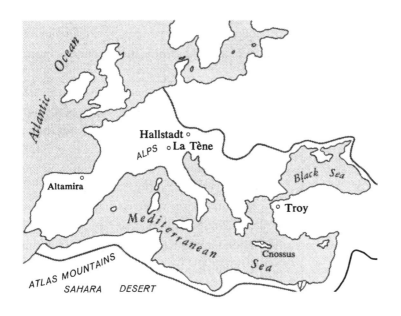

III·THE CALENDAR
OF THE THREE AGES

One of the important consequences of the excavations at Pompeii and Herculaneum was the ability to date not only the objects found in the two towns but similar objects wherever discovered. As the great eruption of Vesuvius occurred in 79 A.D., it followed that all the pottery, coins, and articles of every kind buried under ash and lava must date back to that same year or earlier. But with regard to the dating of other objects, archaeologists were not so fortunate.

One hundred fifty years ago no one so much as dreamed that the earth had existed, and man had lived upon it, for such a vast period. Even though excavators found the evidence of human activity in many places, they could not properly appreciate it.

The importance of the dating problem was evident. In ordinary human relations, a knowledge of the ages of people permits one to answer some fundamental questions about them. If, in a classroom with twenty girls, all but Jane are six and Jane is twenty-six, it does not require the logical ability of an Einstein to deduce that the class is an elementary one and that Jane is the teacher. In the same way, when archaeologists find the remains of several civilizations in contact with each other over a wide area, the ages sometimes tell which civilizations were teachers and which pupils. The problem has come up in Egypt, Sumer, and with regard to the civilization of the Indus Valley in India.

But for a long time it seemed completely insoluble. The geological formations in which archaeological "finds" occur are themselves of extremely uncertain age. For more than a century the best opinions about dating have been no more than guesses, and on occasion very bad guesses. Now, however, we have progressed beyond guesswork. In many cases experts can determine within fairly close limits the actual age of a mummy, a charred log of wood, or a piece of bone.

When archaeology first grew out of a study of antiquities, hardly any one thought of attempting to date an object to the year. Artifacts were described sufficiently when they were designated ancient British, ancient Greek or Roman, or ancient Egyptian. Occasionally a coin or monument which bore the name and image of a king could be ascribed to a definite era, perhaps to a single year. But flints, bones, pieces of pottery, and most other objects of interest to archaeology could not be classified by age at all.

Curiously enough, the first hint of the correct method of dating can be traced back to about 750 B.C., when the Greek poet Hesiod invented a tale which bears an accidental resemblance to the truth. According to Hesiod, man first lived in a Golden Age when the gods smiled upon him. Then divine smiles turned into frowns as he passed through Ages of Silver and Bronze, an Age of Heroes, and finally—in Hesiod's own day, as he gloomily announced—an Age of Iron.

There may well have been in all this some memory of man's actual past, preserved in legends which the poet had heard. If there was, he added to it his personal lamentations for the good old days. To a man who lived when gold was a precious metal, an Age of Gold was obviously superior to one of Iron. But by Hesiod's day the true values of gold and iron were already being forgotten. Gold gave man no aid in his struggle with Nature, while iron was his most useful ally. True, its use ushered in many changes, and led to the gradual destruction of old customs, and this was reason enough for poets to despise it.

For that matter, the common people were as blind as the poets. Even a great historian like Herodotus, who was also a great traveler and had visited many different peoples, could not distinguish fact from fable. Herodotus saw around him survivors of the actual Ages of Man. But though he had sharp eyes and an inquiring mind, he could not interpret properly what he saw. All non-Greeks were to him barbarians.

The minds of men who came later were clouded or closed by ignorance, by superstition, and by the dogmas of those great intellects who told others what to think. They remained closed for more than two thousand years. They were opened finally by collections of flints, swords, arrowheads, and other long useless objects, and by the insight of a few men.

By the beginning of the nineteenth century, large sections of the museums of Europe resembled junk heaps. One of the more important of these vast nondescript collections was in Denmark, where many relics found their way to the National Museum in Copenhagen. What was to be done with them?

So long as they were thought to be elfin arrows, fairy thunderbolts, or similar supernatural paraphernalia, nothing much. Even the more sensible antiquarians, who attributed the old flints and metal weapons to primitive peoples, were at a loss. As they didn't know what primitive peoples had existed, every attempt at classification on this basis soon found itself in just as blind an alley.

A new curator of the Danish National Museum, Christian Jurgensen Thomsen, determined to find some system that would make sense. To do so he had to visit the sites of archaeological discoveries in the field, observe and dig in the Danish peat bogs, and uncover flints and arrowheads himself. Gradually, as he worked, the truth began to dawn on him—so simple a truth that you might imagine it would find immediate acceptance. But the appearance of simplicity was deceptive, and Thomsen's theories did not suddenly convert the heathen gold- and stone-worshipping world of archaeology.

Thomsen observed that at certain sites objects found in different layers differed in a regular and predictable way. The very lowest objects were made of stone, those directly above of copper or bronze, and those still further up of iron. It is a widely accepted principle of geology that when a site has been undisturbed, the lowest layers (or *strata*) formed by deposits of sand or mud are the oldest, and the age decreases as the layers approach the top. By applying this principle, Thomsen at once had the answer to his problem: the articles in his museum were to be classified by the material of which they were made. The Stone Age was most ancient, and was followed first by an Age of Bronze, and then the Age of Iron.

Why were these simple facts not obvious to other archaeologists? For the reason that in many places objects had been mixed in the course of centuries. Sometimes Iron Age men settled at the site of an old village, and in digging new foundations turned up bronze implements which were later mingled in the same stratum of earth with their own. Or heavy rains eroded several layers, washing away the earth and leaving a confused jumble. Even burrowing animals could transfer objects from one stratum to another.

Most important of all were several facts which neither Thomsen nor other archaeologists of his time had the background to understand. Neither the Bronze nor the Iron Age came suddenly in any place, and neither represented a definite time in years. The Iron Age arrived in Asia Minor about 1200 B.C. But for many centuries the Stone Age persisted in parts of Europe, as it continued to persist in other parts of the world into the twentieth century. Moreover, in any one area, tools and weapons continued to be made at the same time of stone and of bronze, or of stone and iron. When stone and iron tools were in the same layer, which Age did they represent?

Thomsen faced other difficulties as well. It was satisfying to have discovered a logical method of classifying objects in a museum. But an object torn away from its surroundings had lost most of its archaeological meaning. Of the thousands of flints and arrowheads and spearheads and drinking cups and other articles in the National Museum—which had been found together? Under what circumstances were they dug up?

Thomsen's classification thus applied in only the most general way to the finds in the National Museum, where he began to bring order out of a chaotic mess in the second decade of the nineteenth century. In 1819 the Museum was opened to the public with the objects classified according to his scheme of the Three Ages, and not long afterward he began to publish details concerning the methods he had used.

Despite all objections, Thomsen's methods did form the basis for scientific archaeology. During the first half of the century, he and other Danish archaeologists emphasized the importance of the Three-Age system. Among the more important names are those of Jens Jacob Worsaae and Sven Nillson. The Danish school of archaeology which Thomsen founded did more, however, than merely classify. It began to remedy the weaknesses which his work had brought to light, to develop techniques of excavation and of recording as well as of interpretation.

As was to be expected, archaeologists in other countries found difficulty in using Thomsen's Three Ages. Objects encountered in certain strata of Danish soil did not occur in similar strata in England, for example, or in Italy. This was clearly a consequence of the fact that different Ages came to different places at different times.

The chief obstacle to the acceptance of Thomsen's system, however, was not so much in the archaeological facts as in the minds of men. The thought that the earth as well as the creatures on it had passed through a continuous series of changes during hundreds of millions of years, and that similar changes had taken place over a shorter period of time in human society seemed fantastic. For most people the Bible was the guide to prehistoric chronology, despite the fact that the Bible was not written as a scientific textbook. One prominent theologian dated the creation of man in the year 4004 B.C., and an eager bishop pinpointed the very moment—9:00 A.M. on October 23rd.

If 4004 B.C. set a limit beyond which the world had not existed, what were archaeologists to make of the bones of ancient mammoths and cave bears and rhinoceroses sometimes found in Europe? What of the tools and human bones occasionally found with them? Nothing at all, except that such finds were a snare and a delusion best left to the devil who had contrived them.

But the civilized world of the nineteenth century was changing with a speed that surprised and shocked the older generation of anti-evolutionists. It became increasingly clear from geological evidence that the human species had existed long before 4004 B.C.

This evidence was distasteful to many people, and as a result of their efforts to make it known, geologists became suspicious characters. In England they aroused the resentment of conservative Britons by writing magazine articles and otherwise unsettling people's minds. In those early days of Queen Victoria's reign, however, the worthy old gentlemen who so hated the coming of change did manage to protect some of the innocent. They prohibited ladies from attending lectures in geology at King's College, in London, and thus exposing their tender minds to dangerous facts about the weathering of rocks, soil erosion, destruction by earthquakes, and other geological forces.

These valiant efforts eventually proved useless. In 1847 the French archaeologist Jacques Boucher de Perthes reported that ancient tools had been found in France together with the remains of extinct animals. The evidence was clear proof of the antiquity of man. Many scholars of the time found a dozen reasons for rejecting it as incredible. And then Boucher de Perthes, trying to uncover additional evidence to support his views, ran into trouble. Knowing of his eagerness to discover human artifacts, his workmen thoughtfully manufactured flint instruments of a primitive type, and with them salted gravel pits where excavation was going on. When the flints were "discovered," Boucher de Perthes was overjoyed—until they were proved to be forgeries.

This was one of the most notorious of the cases of forgery and suspected forgery which have plagued the study of archaeology. It is questionable which has done more harm: the deliberate deception that induces others to accept the false as true, or the unconscious self-delusion which impels a man to reject the true as false. In any case, the uproar about the forged flints cast doubt for a time upon all the evidence laboriously assembled by Boucher de Perthes.

It also made archaeologists forget that this evidence did not stand alone. In many places over the European continent there were strange mounds called "kitchen middens," or kitchen leavings. The mounds, first studied in Denmark by Worsaae, contained pieces of pottery, bones, stone implements, oyster and clam shells, and other refuse. The pottery could have been made only by human hands. But some of the bones with which it was associated were of animals not found in Europe during historic days. It should have been concluded that at least some of the pottery had been made by men who lived before the dawn of written history. The prevailing prejudice, however, did not permit this conclusion to be drawn.

Then, in the dry winter of 1853-54, the waters of Lake Zurich in Switzerland receded sufficiently to give up a secret they had held for centuries. At the town of Obermeilen the remains of wooden piles which had once supported ancient dwellings were uncovered. The astonished eyes of the modern villagers saw for the first time the remains of the lake dwellings in which their own remote ancestors might have lived.

An artist's reproduction of lake dwellings built on logs during the Stone Age
(Switzerland)

A local schoolmaster, Dr. Aeppli, realizing the possible importance of the find and lacking the training to investigate by himself, called in Dr. Ferdinand Keller of Zurich. Excavation under Dr. Keller uncovered stone axes, pottery, charred wood and horn implements, and the remains of animal bones. Once their existence was known, other lake dwellings were sought and found. Of different ages and of various types, they revealed an unsuspected way of life which had once been common in France, Germany, and Italy, as well as in Switzerland. Together with the kitchen middens, whose importance was slowly being realized, the lake dwellings supplied the final evidence in support of Thomsen's system of Three Ages.

Many of these sites had been occupied for a long time, and the remains of different kinds of fruit and grain, of wood and flax fibers, as well as of weapons and animal bones, gave detailed information about the daily lives of the lake dwellers

[31]

and how they had changed as the centuries rolled on. In the meantime, while exploring the caves of southern France with the English banker Henry Christy, the archaeologist Eduard Lartet made an exciting and completely unexpected discovery. Among the objects he picked up was a reindeer bone on which the picture of two horses had been engraved. Dating back to the Stone Age, this reindeer bone showed that the men of that primitive period had possessed an interest in art.

It is amusing to note that these early examples of the cultural strivings of men of the Stone Age were also at first denounced as forgeries. About the same time, other important discoveries were made at La Tène, in Switzerland, and at Hallstadt, in Austria. Both places were the center of Iron Age cultures, La Tène dating from about 54 B.C., Hallstadt from more than 500 years earlier. Each supplied a tremendous amount of evidence about the life of primitive man.

The total impact of the new evidence began to be overwhelming. Diehards continued to protest, but more and more in vain. For in 1858 vindication finally came to Boucher de Perthes. Fissures were discovered in the floor of Brixham Cave in England, along with evidence of human habitation. A distinguished committee was appointed to superintend the excavation and make sure there was no fraud. As the committee included several skeptics who did not believe in the antiquity of man, its findings were certain to command respect. And when the diggers uncovered flint tools, along with the bones of lions, reindeer, bears, mammoths, and rhinoceroses—all of them extinct in England outside of zoos and circuses—the skeptics on the committee saw with their own eyes, confessed the error of their ways, and admitted that their previous opinions had been somewhat prejudiced.

The following year, 1859, saw the publication of Charles

Darwin's *The Origin of Species,* a book which presented overwhelming evidence in favor of the theory of evolution and produced a tremendous change in the climate of opinion of the
scientific world. Now old as well as recently discovered facts
could be regarded with a new and clearer vision. Thomsen's
theory of the Three Ages spread throughout Europe, and as is
so often the ironic fate of scientific theories, once it was whole-
heartedly accepted by the majority, its weaknesses became increasingly apparent. Stone implements, for example, differed
from each other so much that clearly there was no single Stone
Age—there were Stone Ages. How many? That was a matter
for further argument. At least, however, man had glimpsed
something of his past, and was beginning to realize that he
was no newcomer on the terrestrial scene.

The question remained: exactly how old was he? Was it
possible that the Stone, Bronze, and Iron Ages had all flitted by
within the few thousand years that anti-evolutionists were
willing to grant the human race? To this second question
archaeologists replied with a definite "No." The divisions of
the Stone Age alone must obviously have lasted many thousands of years. Moreover, in 1856, bones of a strange skeleton
had been discovered in the Neander Valley in Germany. They
were obviously human, and yet differed from the human bones
of today. At first only part of a skull and some long bones
were found, but these were enough to indicate that Neanderthal
Man, as he soon came to be known, had a weak chin, heavy
jaw, and sloping forehead. He seemed much more apelike
than present-day man.

To some zoologists, Neanderthal Man was an ancestor, or
at least a forerunner, of modern man. "Nonsense," retorted
various eminent experts. Neanderthal Man was quite modern,
and the bones were not ancient at all. The poor fellow had

merely been mentally deficient, hence the strange shape of his skull, and he had suffered from rheumatism, which explained the misshapen legs.

But these explanations left many archaeologists unconvinced. And as time went on, and more of these strange bones were found, it became clear that Neanderthal Man *was* ancient, of a racial type unknown to any historic people. He must have lived and died out many thousands of years before even the Egyptians came on the stage of history.

It was still impossible to guess *how* many. That, however, did not prevent archaeologists from trying to subdivide the Stone Age according to relative antiquity. Eduard Lartet, for example, devised a charming, if short-lived system based on the predominant type of animal. According to Lartet, the early part of the Stone Age was the Cave Bear period, followed by the period of the Woolly Mammoth or Rhinoceros, the Reindeer period, and finally the period of the Aurochs or Ancient Bison. But the archaeological data did not fit well into this classification, and it did not win wide acceptance.

As archaeological digging went on, Gabriel de Mortillet, a pupil of Lartet's gave up his master's animal arrangements and suggested a scheme that was more modest, if less picturesque. Why not name the finds simply after the site where they were uncovered? By now Thomsen's original Stone Age had been subdivided into Paleolithic, or Old Stone Age, and Neolithic, or New Stone Age. Gabriel de Mortillet subdivided the Old Stone Age into four periods named after different regions in France. To these were soon added an Eolithic, or "Dawn Stone Age," before the Paleolithic, and the Mesolithic, or "Middle Stone Age," between the Paleolithic and Neolithic.

This new classification also had its weaknesses. Excavation often uncovered many layers at one site. This meant that each of De Mortillet's periods had to be subdivided. It then became evident that there was overlapping between different periods, and, still worse, that some of these subdivisions had no exact counterparts in large areas of Europe.

The very wealth of archaeological finds was creating new confusion. Vast numbers of flint and metal arrow and axe heads, of bone and ivory implements, of shells from ancient oysters and clams, and endless pieces of pottery filled archaeological collections. The order which Thomsen had imposed by his system of Three Ages was breaking down. It was time for a new insight which would once more permit archaeologists to find their way as if with a time-compass among the different centuries of man's ancient history.

Examples of engraving and sculpture representing cultures of the later Paleolithic Age

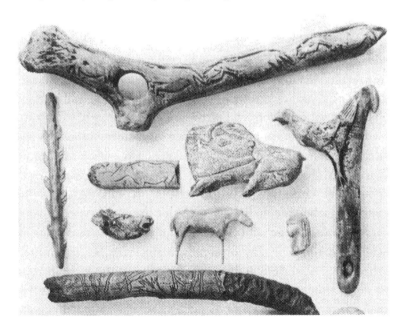

IV-THE CALENDARS
OF SCIENCE

THE NEW INSIGHT INTO THE CLASSIFICATION OF ARCHAEOLOGICAL finds came from Gustave Oscar Montelius, born in Sweden in 1842. Montelius gradually evolved a method of matching dates by "types." The principle of the method was simple enough, although its practical application required a tremendous amount of work. If a given type of pottery, for instance, occurred in geological strata in two different areas, one might reasonably assume that the pottery had been made in the same period and the strata deposited at roughly the same time. But what articles were to be considered as being of the same type? Urns made on a potter's wheel and those fashioned entirely by hand, for instance, were obviously different. But if two kinds of pottery were made by wheel in the same way, showed the same design and pattern of decoration, and so on, they might be accepted as examples of the same type.

Montelius applied his method of typing to metal objects as well as to those of clay or stone. In this way he determined what strata of different sites corresponded to the same period of development and eventually extended the method to international matching of types. Once he had shown that daggers, or flint knives, or clay urns of different countries belonged to the same age, he could turn his attention to objects found with the daggers, knives, or urns, whether these other objects were of gold, stone, clay, or any other material. Different types found together defined a *culture,* which represented a given period almost as definitely as the individual types did. If cultures A and B included bronze daggers of the same type, they represented the same subdivision of the Bronze Age. Excavators might find no daggers in culture C. But if they came across the same kind of pottery in culture C as in culture B, B and C also represented the same period in the Bronze Age.

By this process of checking on types and cultures Montelius was able to begin the work of matching Bronze Age periods in Europe with those of Egyptian ruling families, or *dynasties.* He did not, as he himself realized, completely solve the problem of age. Not knowing how long ago the Egyptian dynasties had existed, Montelius couldn't date either Egyptian or Bronze Age cultures in Europe.

Later on, as more and more historical records were discovered, the order in which different kings had ascended the throne and the duration of their reigns were well worked out. Historical records in themselves could not supply absolute dates, but many of the old texts and inscriptions referred to astronomical events, and in particular to one important event that marked the beginning of the Egyptian year. This was the heliacal rising of the star, Sirius; that is, the first appearance of this bright star at sunrise after a long period during which it had been invisible. From the records of heliacal risings astronomers were able to fix the first absolute dates for the beginning of the Twelfth Dynasty, about 2000 B.C., and the beginning of the Eighteenth Dynasty, about 1580 B.C., with a possible error of three or four years. As the Egyptian dynasties were matched with culture periods in Crete, an island near Greece, and Sumer, in the Near East, it became possible to date events in these regions as well.

However, literary references were not always so helpful. And as excavators uncovered bones and artifacts from before the time when literature existed, they were more and more forced back to the method of geological estimates, which were often seriously in error.

Now came a striking advance. Another Swedish scientist, Baron Gerard de Geer, by his brilliant observations discovered what most archaeologists had despaired of finding, an *absolute* method of dating events. He knew that at one time most of Europe had been covered by an ice sheet. Every year the melting water from glacial ice had laid down a deposit in regular order. During the spring and summer thaw, the water flowing from the ice had formed rivulets, and these had merged into larger streams capable of carrying not only fine soil but also gravel and even pebbles. As the streams left the ice behind, they spread out, and their flow became sluggish. First they dropped the pebbles, then the gravel, next the coarser particles of sand, and finally the particles of clay. The result was a deposit of characteristic structure. A year's deposit might be thicker or thinner from one season to the next—but each set of layers, called a *varve,* represented a year.

Therefore, starting with the present time at the edge of the ice sheet, all that was needed was to count back layer by layer to determine the age of each varve.

In practice, even such a simple and brilliant idea as this faced difficulties. Occasionally more than one varve was deposited in a single year. And in some regions the deposits of hundreds of years were missing, worn away by erosion. Baron de Geer and his students traveled up and down the Scandinavian coast to measure the layers that could be found in each area and match them with other areas. Eventually they constructed a fairly reliable "varve calendar." Even though it wasn't perfect, it could be used to set absolute dates for events which previously could be dated only relatively.

The varve calendar gave dates as far back as 10,000 B.C.—time enough to include all the dynasties of Egypt and the entire Neolithic Age everywhere in the world. Unfortunately, however, the method of dating by artifact types was needed to match Scandinavian finds with those of other countries—and types did not provide a year to year match between different areas. Moreover, over large portions of the globe types were not matched at all with neighboring areas. For these reasons, dating by the combined use of typology and the varve calendar was seriously limited.

Another Swede, Lennart von Post, later found a way to overcome some of the weaknesses of previous dating methods. During a good part of the year, the air is filled with plant pollen. This fine dust from the stamens of flowers consists of numerous tiny cells needed to fertilize female plants, and it resists destruction by weather and time even better than some of the "everlasting rocks" which poets and philosophers have talked about. In peat bogs and in soils all over the world, grains of pollen deposited hundreds and thousands of years ago have maintained their form and structure.

Each type of pollen cell, easily recognizable (by experts, that is) under the microscope, bears witness to the plant from which it came. And at any period, the plants of a particular region reveal the nature of the climate during their lifetimes. By counting the different kinds of pollen in a layer of peat and using these data to calculate the percentages of different plants that grew in the area, botanists could create a picture of the forests which then existed, match this against known data about forest composition, and date the time of deposition of the peat. As every artifact was dug up with some earth clinging to it, and this earth almost always contained plant remains, it could thus be dated.

To the pollen dating method, archaeologists soon added another botanical aid, known as *dendrochronology*. This is simply the fixing of dates by counting tree rings. At first glance it would appear that the oldest date that could be determined in any area depended on the oldest tree of that area still alive, or known to have died at a definite time. If a botanist knew that a certain redwood, for instance, was struck by lightning and killed five years ago, he could count the rings of its trunk and determine how long ago it developed from a seed, in this way setting a date of perhaps a thousand years back. But before that?

As it happens, it is possible to extend the use of dendrochronology into the past far beyond the life of any single tree. The temperature and rainfall in a region vary from year to year, and these variations are reflected in the appearance of tree rings. Any given series of rings forms a characteristic pattern, and by matching the pattern of the early years of a young redwood with that of the late years of a redwood that died perhaps eight hundred years ago, and so on, botanists can trace tree rings further and further into the past. In California, where long-lived redwoods grow, dating can be extended to beyond 1000 B.C. And by matching tree ring patterns with similar patterns in logs used for ancient buildings, archaeologists can date the buildings as well. The method is reliable but not always applicable. It can be used only where variations in rainfall cause marked changes in tree growth, or the tree ring patterns may be impossible to match.

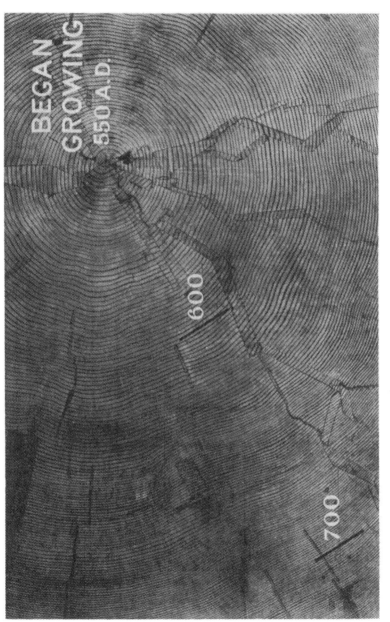

BEGAN GROWING 550 A.D.

600

700

A cross-section, in close-up, of a Sequoia tree cut in 1891. The rings tell us that the tree started to grow in 550 A.D.

Useful as these methods are, they all suffer from serious limitations, some of which have been indicated. There is one method, however, unsuspected until the nineteen-forties, which gives absolute dates as far back as twenty-five thousand years ago, and is applicable to any area in the world. This is a method based on carbon-14.

For many thousands of years, possibly for all the billions of its existence, our earth has been receiving visitors from the far reaches of space—not living visitors, but tiny particles laden with enormous energies. Thought to have come from *super-novae*—distant stars which flare up suddenly to billions of times their previous brilliance—and known as cosmic rays, these particles have for ages raced along at almost the speed of light. On reaching our planet they plow through its atmosphere and break up, their fragments crashing along the way into nitrogen atoms and transforming the nitrogen into a heavy form of carbon called carbon-14. The newly formed atoms are radioactive. They decay so slowly that only half of them are gone in about 5,568 years. By measuring the rate of decay of any sample of carbon we can thus learn what proportion of it is carbon-14.

For a time archaeologists saw no connection between these facts and the problem of dating. But physicists and radiochemists who worked with carbon-14 began to test some curious theories.

What happened to the carbon-14 produced by cosmic rays? Chemically it was like ordinary carbon and formed carbon dioxide in the atmosphere. From the atmosphere it was absorbed into the bodies of plants, later to become part of animals which ate the plants.

When a plant or animal died, its body disintegrated and carbon dioxide went back to the atmosphere. But if by some unusual circumstance part of the body remained intact, the carbon-14 remained in it, the amount decreasing slowly by ordinary radioactive decay.

By measuring the ratio of carbon-14 to ordinary carbon, then, radiochemists could calculate the length of time during which radioactive decay took place. By analyzing a piece of wood, for instance, they could determine how many years had passed since this wood was part of a living tree.

For the confirmation of these theories, many difficult experiments were needed. W. F. Libby, who headed the group of scientists working on the dating project, obtained samples of wood not only from modern plants but from the tombs of Egyptian Pharaohs and ancient Hittites, as well as from other sources. The dates of the tombs were known from historical records. Analysis for carbon-14 gave results in agreement with the dates already known.

The method seemed to work, and soon the archaeologists were intensely interested. Out of the blue sky had come a method that was powerful and correct. It couldn't tell that an event happened precisely 2,357 years, 3 months, and 7 days ago. It *could* tell that the date was 2,400 plus or minus 300. It fixed the time of early man in America as beyond ten thousand, not a mere two thousand or five thousand years. It offered answers to dating problems before which tree-ring and pollen methods were completely helpless.

No wonder then that carbon-14 laboratories sprang up in Europe and the United States. With their help archaeologists at last began to put in order a valid timetable of the development of man in different parts of the globe. Two wandering Arabs had discovered the Dead Sea Scrolls. Were they genuine remains of antiquity or, as some people darkly hinted, carefully contrived fakes? Analyses for carbon-14 helped prove that they were genuine remains. Pieces of linen in which the

Scrolls had been wrapped were approximately two thousand years old, and the age of the linen helped fix the age of the Scrolls.

The radiocarbon method is not infallible. For a sample of linen or charred bone to be dated correctly it must have lain untouched by nature or by human hands. If it has undergone long soaking in ground water, for instance, carbon dioxide dissolved in the water may have modified the radiocarbon content of the sample. For this and similar reasons, determining a radiocarbon date is not as easy as reading a wall calendar.

It is nevertheless necessary to emphasize once more the power of the method when properly used. When combined with methods which measure the content of other radioactive elements in rocks, it may extend the dating of geological as well as archaeological records back to the beginning of man on earth, and far beyond.

For archaeologists of the future, however, who may wish to date the present era, the carbon-14 method may be useless. One assumption on which the method is based is the constancy of the atmosphere's carbon-14 content. This assumption is no longer strictly valid. The explosion of atomic bombs has already increased the amount of atmospheric carbon-14, and peaceful uses of atomic energy will increase it still further. In case of atomic war, carbon-14 values, like everything else, would go sky-high. If there *are* any archaeologists of the future, they will not be able to date our era by whatever carbon-containing remains survive.

But the work of present-day archaeologists is less concerned with the future than the past. Let us see what other help they have received from other sciences.

V - THE SISTER SCIENCES

THE CARBON-14 DATING METHOD IS ONE OF THE MOST UNEXPECTED
and generous dividends ever paid by one branch of science to
another. Let us consider other such dividends.

The foundations of civilization are generally believed to
have been born about 3,500 to 3,000 B.C. They may have originated, as most present-day archaeologists believe, between the
Tigris and Euphrates rivers in Mesopotamia, or may have had
independent origins in Egypt and India. The evidence present-
ly available is not conclusive. But man did enter the Bronze
Age and begin to build cities during this period in the Near
East, and many skills he acquired here did spread to other
areas.

[45]

Why the Near East? Why didn't civilization flourish during this period in North Africa, Greece, or Southern Italy? Of the answers usually given, many emphasize the importance of the food supply. In Mesopotamia it was possible for even the most primitive farmers to produce crops so abundant that man could leave hunting behind and turn to agriculture. The fertility of Mesopotamian soil was legendary in the ancient world. Herodotus noted it in his *History* and other Greeks envied it. But this answer leads to another question: why was the soil so fertile? Why, despite centuries of farming, was it not exhausted, like the soil of the Mayas in Central America?

At this point the botanists and bacteriologists step in with a slightly technical but fascinating explanation.

One of the plants that grow wild in Iraq is known to botanists as *Prosopis stephaniana*. A perennial plant, it has long roots which anchor it firmly to the ground, and like the human race itself, it thrives in the desert as well as in open fields, near river banks, and on mountain foothills. It has long roots in another sense as well, for its history goes back at least 5,000 years. In ancient Mesopotamia, both Sumerians and Akkadians had words for it, and probably so did the prehistoric peoples before them.

On the long roots of *Prosopis* are little knots of *Rhizobium* bacteria. These take nitrogen out of the air and in this way add large stores of nitrate to the soils of the Tigris and Euphrates valleys. Without nitrate as fertilizer, plants become stunted and die. With the nitrate supplied by *Rhizobium* bacteria on the roots of *Prosopis,* fertility is restored. In the fields of Mesopotamia this fertility lasted over three millennia to be destroyed only within the last thousand years or so. The relation between these beneficent bacteria, the wild plant, and the origin of civilization is therefore of some importance.

This sort of investigation is disconcerting to archaeologists who find their work already complicated enough without having to learn bacteriology. They are well aware that botany has contributed pollen dating and dendrochronology. Now they must take account of its other services as well. There can be little progress in studying the development of man without noting his dependence on his environment. Man has always lived upon plants, for if they do not feed him directly, they at least feed the animals that feed him. A branch of botany is therefore investigating this relation between man and his plant environment, and is already shedding light on his early development.

It is interesting to examine further the question of how civilization began. What was the crop that benefited so greatly from the fertility of Mesopotamian soil? Chiefly wheat, which has always been the great food plant of the West. Wheat now grows all over the world, but its numerous varieties appear to be derived from two species of wild grasses found in Southwest Asia. During the several thousand years that separated the beginning of the Neolithic or New Stone Age from the Bronze Age, wheat reached the fertile soil of the Near East and began to play its historic role of man's chief food. Without the two wild grasses, there would have been no civilization.

Let us go on to another science. For years archaeologists have used chemical methods to help in their study of artifacts, and now they are more dependent on chemistry than ever. Analysis can show easily enough, for example, whether a bone is fossil or modern. As a bone ages it loses its organic matter, that is, its carbon, its closely bound water, and its nitrogen. Even as far back as 1863, therefore, chemical analysis was able to prove forgery in fossils. In that year chemists showed that a jaw planted with faked flints by the workmen of Boucher de

Perthes had the nitrogen content of modern bone and was therefore fraudulent, along with the flints.

By the year 1948 another chemical method of approximate dating was available, more sensitive than the method of nitrogen analysis. It consisted of analysis for the element fluorine. As bones lie in the ground, water continually seeps through them, so that over the years the mineral matter in the bone absorbs fluorine, even though only a few atoms from each drop of water. Thus the fluorine content of fossils increases with age. The method is not accurate enough to serve for dating in the same way that carbon-14 analysis does. But it can tell easily enough the difference between bones a hundred or a thousand years old and a million. Also it can testify whether different specimens found together actually belong together. For instance, human and animal bones found in the same area in a long dried Texas lake have been shown to have the same fluorine content. These early Texans therefore lived about the same time as the animals, and possibly hunted them to their deaths.

An even more recently developed method depends on the analysis of bones for small amounts of what are called "amino acids." These acids are derived from the protein of bones. By analyzing the traces of amino acids left, the chemist can set an approximate date for the time when the animal was alive. Again the calendar provided by amino-acid analysis is not as accurate as that of carbon-14. But it extends further back into the past, as far back as twenty-five million years or more.

Another interesting application of "paleochemistry," or the chemistry of ancient objects, is in determining blood types. Human beings differ slightly from each other in almost every detail of blood chemistry, and all can be classified in four main blood types, with many minor subdivisions. Blood type can be determined from a single drop of blood, even from blood that was shed centuries before. Paleochemists have begun to study the bones of American Indians of ten thousand or more years ago as well as those of Egyptian mummies, and have been able in both cases to determine blood types. As these are inherited according to definite laws, it is possible to some extent to determine human relationships from them, among primitive peoples no less than among modern parents and children. Archaeologists interested in tracing the migrations of these peoples may in the future accomplish their aim by analyzing blood types found in different areas and noting how the patterns change as different peoples meet.

Meanwhile chemistry has already provided considerable help in other ways in outlining the travels of ancient man. It has, for example, helped chart the trade routes of the Bronze Age. Archaeologists have found in different countries bronze objects very like those made in Egypt or Asia Minor about four thousand years ago. Did different races make similar objects, perhaps learning the art of working bronze from each other, or were the objects themselves imported over regular trade routes? Bronze is an alloy of copper and tin, but it also contains small amounts of other metals, and all the objects made in the same way in one area during a given period have about the same chemical composition. Therefore, analysis of tiny shavings has been used to decide whether different bronze objects originated in the same place. On plotting the geographical pattern of objects from a common source, it is then possible to obtain a record of the travels of primitive merchants.

New methods have recently been developed for analyzing pottery and bronze without even the need for chipping off tiny fragments or for using shavings. A piece of pottery may be studied with X-rays, or subjected to the action of an atomic pile.

In the latter case, tiny electrically neutral particles called neutrons bombard the object and change some of its atoms into radioactive forms. Measurements of the different kinds of radioactivity produced establish the identity and quantity of many of the chemical elements present.

Chemistry also suggests sites for excavation. We have already seen that without proper nutrients, such as nitrate, plants cannot grow. Of equal importance with nitrate is phosphate. If a soil contains enough phosphate, it will support considerable plant growth, as well as a large number of animals which eat the plants. At the site of human habitation (provided there is no sewage or garbage disposal system) the phosphate that comes from the surrounding region will be consumed by human beings and excreted in a limited area. Here the phosphate content of the soil continually increases, and phosphate analysis can therefore suggest, even without other evidence, that human beings once lived here.

It would be difficult to name a science that in one way or another has *not* helped archaeology in the past or is unlikely to help it in the future. Modern archaeologists tend to look at their science as a set of techniques and methods used to investigate problems that arise in other fields of inquiry. If they are interested in the civilizations of Greece, Crete, Egypt, Rome, or Mesopotamia, they usually think of themselves as *historians.* If they study the archaeology of prehistory, they consider themselves *anthropologists.* For this reason archaeology is often considered a branch of anthropology and in many universities is taught in the anthropology department.

Those anthropologists who study the more or less primitive tribes or nations who have survived into our own time are *ethnologists,* and archaeologists apply the insight their colleagues have gained to the ways of thinking of races long dead.

The discoveries of cave paintings of animals, for instance, and of primitive graves containing the remains of food, testify to a belief in magic and in life after death, and studies of modern tribes confirm this interpretation. In general, ethnology has been a useful guide, even though it must be used with caution, and its findings about people in one land do not necessarily apply to those of another far separated in space or time.

Many sciences which at first sight would appear to have little importance for archaeology have shown themselves closely related. Oceanography, for instance, is of great possible value. Objects are now being recovered from long sunken ships as well as from underwater soil deposits, and a knowledge of currents, tides, changes in chemical composition of sea water, and other intimate details of the ocean's behavior promises to shed new light on what happened thousands of years ago.

What of volcanology, that relatively isolated specialty which treats of the lives and habits of volcanoes? Well, special fields of human knowledge are never as isolated as they seem. Take two such lonely sciences as volcanology and dendrochronology, arrange a marriage, and some strange offspring result.

The year 1783 was, as Benjamin Franklin noted, a year of constant fog all over Europe and a great part of North America. It was a queer dry fog which the sun's rays could not break up, and was almost certainly caused by volcanic dust. In June of that year Iceland had a violent volcanic eruption and two months later Japan underwent "the most frightful eruption on record." That year the harvest was bad in Finland, and extremely hot south winds swept through central Europe all summer. In some places, when winter finally came, it was the worst in the memory of the oldest inhabitants.

The unusual weather that resulted from the volcanic fog produced, in Alaska, Scandinavia, and northern Europe generally, tree rings of a most unusual nature, extremely easy to identify. The importance of this fact is twofold. First, it shows that the system of dendrochronology has given correct data for Alaska at least as far back as 1783. Second, it indicates that other great eruptions, which like those of 1783 spread dust particles over the earth's entire atmosphere but have never been recorded, can be detected and dated by their similar action on the nature of tree rings.

In this way, evidence of a nature once totally unsuspected can be used to extend our knowledge further and further back into the past. There are great and yawning gaps in the archaeological record. Slowly, from the testimony of such inanimate witnesses as tree stumps, slumbering volcanoes, and long-buried layers of soil, the gaps are being filled in.

What of zoology? The zoology of ancient life that we study is naturally the zoology of those parts of animals which have survived—the bones, teeth, horns, antlers, occasional shreds of hair and skin, and so on. Limited as such remains are, they are still of such importance that special textbooks on bone, for example, are written for archaeologists. And when zoology is combined with the branch of mathematics called statistics, it has even more to offer. Throughout many areas of the world, in caves and villages which have been the scene of long human habitation, the bones of the animals men have eaten have accumulated over the centuries. A statistical analysis of bone types yields interesting and important information. If the bones found are those of wild animals, the men who ate them were obviously hunters and were in the Old Stone Age. If the bones are mostly of domestic animals, they were eaten by New Stone Age or still more advanced groups. From a study of bones it is possible to learn which animals man has domesticated at any stage, and how their domestication affected his way of life.

It has already become evident that geology is to the archaeologist a science of fundamental importance. Any scientist engaged in excavations must know the structure of the geological formations among which he is working. It helps him too if he knows whether a region was subject to earthquakes or volcanic action and if he has geologic evidence of floods and the action of glaciers.

Linguistics, a branch of the science which studies languages, has provided interesting clues to the men who seek to learn about ancient cultures. English and most modern European and Asian languages, including French, Spanish, Dutch, German, Polish, Russian, Bulgarian, Icelandic, Gaelic, and many others, as well as ancient Greek, Latin, Sanskrit, and Hittite, were all derived originally from one parent tongue. By comparing the transformations which words have undergone in different regions of Europe and Asia, linguists have succeeded to a limited extent in reconstructing the original Indo-European language. More important to their archaeological friends, from the presence of words referring to certain plants and animals, as well as to family relationships, they have been able to deduce facts about the customs and culture of the primitive people who spoke the language.

The methods of cryptography, the science of deciphering codes and ciphers, have been of great value. So for that matter have been the methods of criminology. The archaeological successors of Sherlock Holmes have found a field wide open to their talents in more important cases than Sherlock ever tackled.

Among the most valuable assistants that archaeology has acquired in the past forty years is the science of aerodynamics combined with photography. In the early days of the nineteenth century, archaeologists made plaster casts of objects they could not take with them, or had sketches made by artists. But with the development of photography, artists were supplanted to some extent. However, it is still true that an artist's sketch can show finer details, and while photographs of complicated designs can be taken more rapidly than any artist can sketch, both forms of recording finds are needed. In the latter third of the nineteenth century the photographer became an indispensable member of every archaeological expedition, but most expeditions include draughtsmen as well.

Then along came the aviator. It was discovered in World War I that many details invisible to a person standing among them on the ground were clearly outlined to a man looking down from about a thousand feet. During the war itself aerial reconnaissance was concerned naturally enough with military objectives. But it revealed much of archaeological interest as well. Outlines of ancient fields uncultivated since Roman times, of picket fences long since turned to dust, of stone buildings fallen centuries before were all distinguishable by the lines and patterns they had left on the ground, and could be photographed from above.

After the war, research in aerial photography for archaeological purposes was continued, especially as it became apparent that discoveries of great geological value, both from the commercial and scientific points of view, could be made by the same methods. It was chiefly for the geologist's sake that high-altitude and stereoscopic color photography were developed to reveal details over wide areas. The slow and laborious search for excavation sites which had once been part of almost every expedition's program became unnecessary. Now a study of aerial photographs permits archaeologists to select with amazing accuracy the sites of ancient cities and burial places.

Almost every advance in electronics is sooner or later reflected in archaeological studies. Electronic "brains" have been used to fill in missing portions of the Dead Sea Scrolls. These same brains—or computers, to use a neutral word—are now being constructed to translate from one modern language, such as Russian or Italian, into another. They can also be applied to the more rapid and accurate classification of the symbols and symbol combinations of an as yet untranslated language. They do not do away with the need for human brains, but they do lend valuable and untiring assistance, and thus permit archaeologists to solve difficult problems more efficiently.

Electronic devices have also helped in the study of objects that lie beneath the surface of a lake or ocean or ordinary soil. They have even been used in combination with a new underground camera for the exploration of Etruscan tombs.

Italian archaeologists have long been in a losing race with tomb robbers. The Etruscans, who flourished twenty-five hundred years ago, made the same mistake as the Egyptian Pharaohs: they supplied their dead with objects of such value that thieves began to carry them off. As there have always been more thieves than archaeologists, the latter were at a serious disadvantage. The use of scientific methods, however, has at last enabled them to overcome their handicap.

First an aerial survey is carried out to locate a number of Etruscan tombs. No time is wasted in completely excavating each individual tomb, which would take a long time and might not yield worthwhile finds. Instead, the center of each tomb is located by the use of electronic echo sounders, and then a small hole is drilled into the earth and stone above the center. A miniature "needle" camera and electronic flashgun are now introduced into this hole, and when the camera reaches the area of chief interest, the pressing of a button sets it going. It revolves automatically, taking a series of color photographs of the interior of the tomb. A study of these photographs at once reveals whether the tomb deserves priority in excavation.

Part of an Etruscan wall in Tarquinia

In this way archaeologists can speed up their work twenty-five or thirty times and gain the upper hand over the tomb robbers —at least until the robbers also adopt scientific methods. This, unfortunately, they are already doing. Thieves equipped as "frogmen" are reported to have gone underwater to rob an Etruscan tomb at the mouth of the River Po.

The speed of advance in other sciences is so great that the archaeologist may be pardoned if he cannot keep up with all the newer discoveries. Certainly he cannot himself know all the devices and methods which may be useful to him. But he must have a good idea of how useful other sciences can be. He must be able to work as a member of a scientific team, and remain alert to the possibilities of new inventions and discoveries in areas of science of which he may never before have heard. As he studies ancient man he must keep up with the most modern approaches, or else he will be left behind and himself become a fossil fit only for some other archaeologist to study.

To take a very important example: chemical, biological, and physical analysis may be indispensable in deciding whether a set of finds is authentic or fraudulent, for frauds and hoaxes, although known in other sciences, are so common in archaeology that they are considered a plague. As an extreme exhibit, there is the striking example of "Piltdown Man."

On December 18, 1912, Arthur Smith-Woodward, a distinguished geologist and paleontologist, together with Charles Dawson, a successful lawyer, announced an exciting find. Dawson had reported to Smith-Woodward the discovery, at Piltdown, in Sussex, England, of part of a skull which apparently belonged to the so-called "missing link" between ape and man. Later a fragment of jawbone was uncovered in the presence of Smith-Woodward. The skull was essentially human, the jawbone, in which two teeth of human type remained, was apelike.

It was exactly what many students of Darwin's theory of evolution had hoped to find. Along with these bones were several flint instruments, including primitive "eoliths," or "dawnstones," and teeth of a hippopotamus, beaver, deer, and horse.

The importance of this discovery immediately made the reputations of the two men. There were skeptics, however, from the first. Some of these did not believe that the skull and jawbone belonged to the same individual. They demanded more evidence. The two teeth in the jaw were molars, considerably worn down by use. It would have been important to find a canine, or eye-tooth. It would also have been important to make a more complete search at Piltdown.

Other searches were in fact made, and in August 1913, Dawson turned up with a canine tooth of exactly the right kind to match the molars. In 1914 a fossil elephant bone shaped like a club was discovered. And in 1915, two miles away from the first site, another Piltdown skull and tooth were picked up, along with a fossil rhinoceros tooth.

The most important scientists in the field of human evolution were convinced. Nevertheless, some of the skeptics were not silenced. For the most part, however, their views were disregarded in England. In the United States, Piltdown Man was regarded as a discovery about which something was wrong.

Dawson died in 1916, and with his death the discoveries at Piltdown came to an end. As time went on, however, discoveries of apelike men were made in other parts of the world —in Java, in China, and in South Africa. The more complete the picture of human evolution became, the less Piltdown Man fitted into it. In all these other primitive human beings, it was the jaws and teeth which became human at an early stage, while their skulls for a long time remained apelike, and only slowly grew in brain capacity.

In 1948, 1949, and 1953 samples of the Piltdown skull and jawbone were analyzed for fluorine. The analyses only made confusion worse. For both had so low a fluorine content that they were obviously much less ancient than had been supposed. The jawbone, in fact, had fluorine in barely detectable amounts, as if it had never been buried in the earth at all.

In 1953, after weighing the evidence, Professor A. S. Weiner came to the distasteful conclusion that somehow there might have been fraud involved. The human origin of the jaw had been indicated by the flat wear of the teeth. But these teeth were worn down far too much. The canine was actually immature, as if from an incompletely grown individual, and yet it too was heavily worn down, indicating a long lifetime of use! What if it had been ground down artificially?

Once the possibility of fraud had been suggested to the right man, the answers were not long in coming. The Piltdown specimens were examined under a microscope, and subjected to both X-ray and chemical analysis. Sections were also cut for examination with the electron microscope, a fascinating instrument which uses a beam of electrons, or negative particles, instead of a beam of light, and can magnify a hundred thousand times or more. The crystal structure of the bones and teeth was determined, and radioactivity studies were made. Objects lying together in the ground for century after century acquire the same degree of radioactivity. If they come from different sites, the difference in radioactivity will betray that fact.

The relative ages of different bone and tooth fragments were determined in several ways, including analysis for organic carbon, organic water, and nitrogen. We may summarize the results very briefly: every object examined proved to be a fraud, deliberately planted at the Piltdown sites! The original skull turned out to be indeed human, but no more than fifty thousand years old, not the million or so first believed, and the jawbone was actually modern, apparently from an orangutan. The teeth had been ground and the jawbone and fossils had been artificially stained. The fossil club of elephant bone had been faked. The animal remains had originally been found elsewhere.

The forger had been a clever man and had used great skill in carrying out his plans. But he was no master criminal who had committed a perfect archaeological crime. He had, it turned out, been extremely lucky, and it was luck as much as skill that had saved him from exposure.

Professor Weiner discovered that as far back as 1912 or 1913 several men had actually suggested fraud. One man had told some of his friends of his suspicions, and had left notes accusing Dawson of forging the Piltdown evidence.

We have seen that as far back as 1863, analysis for nitrogen revealed the fraudulent nature of the jawbone planted by the workmen of Boucher de Perthes. A similar revelation could have taken place in 1912, if eminent scientists had been more aware of the importance of chemical evidence. At the town of Uckfield, the Public Analyst had been given a sample of skull to analyze, and found it free of organic matter. If he had only been given a sample of jawbone as well, he would have shown at once that the jawbone and skull were of different ages.

In this and other respects the forger was lucky to escape detection and exposure in 1912 or 1913. The proof of his identity is not complete, but forty years later circumstantial evidence overwhelmingly indicated that Charles Dawson was deeply involved.

As Professor Weiner points out, the study of the so-called "Piltdown Man" wasted a tremendous amount of energy—almost as much energy as was spent on all the legitimate ape-man fossils put together. It is a prime warning of the danger of neglecting a genuine scientific study of archaeological finds.

Some archaeologists (though not any affiliated with anthropology) have admitted that their subject is greatly dependent on science and makes use of science, but assert that it is not itself a science. They are already far behind the times. For archaeology cannot simply "use" chemistry and botany and physical anthropology and metallurgy as convenient handmaids. A self-respecting science is no one's handmaid.

This opinion has been expressed very sharply by scientists themselves, who have asserted that "when a zoologist identifies a collection of animal bones or a botanist identifies plant remains from an archaeological site," the specialist is as much interested in the ancient environment as is the archaeologist. The point is worth emphasizing. Consider the case of an archaeologist who discovers several pieces of charred wood which he wishes dated by the carbon-14 method, or a selection of plant or animal remains which he wants analyzed. Carbon-14 dating is a tedious and difficult method which requires a high degree of analytical skill, and a scientist who has specialized in this method will not apply this skill, along with his broad general knowledge of the subject, to carry out analyses for the mere purpose of satisfying someone else's curiosity. He will take the trouble to carry out analyses only if they are pertinent to a problem in which he himself is interested, if they become part of his own scientific investigations.

The plant and bone analyst feels the same way. One ethnobotanical laboratory has reported a backlog of unidentified specimens that may take fifteen years to examine, and many experts on bones face similar formidable projects. But again no genuine scientist will devote years of his life to a tedious process of measuring and identifying one bone after another for the sake of an archaeologist who regards him as a mere assistant. Besides, assistants are paid, and the archaeologist, even if he handed over his entire salary, would have trouble hiring one for fifteen years. The scientist will tackle a tedious job only as a collaborator of equal rank.

The basis for this collaboration exists, however, only if the archaeologist regards his own work as part of a science having connections with other sciences. As one scientist, Volney Jones, put it: "An archaeologic site is a unique historical document not only for the development of culture, but for a segment of the history of the earth; archaeologists have no need or desire to reserve these records for themselves, particularly when the culture that is recorded is less impressive or less significant than the noncultural remains. . . . Many sites should in principle be excavated by botanists or zoologists who could send the artifacts to 'cultural archaeologists' for identification."

This is putting the shoe on the other foot with a vengeance, and to many old-fashioned archaeologists it proves a most uncomfortable fit. For now it is they who are being asked to serve as specialist assistants to scientists in the other fields.

There is no disgrace in this. A site whose chief importance lies in its geology, botany, or zoology should be studied by a geologist, botanist, or zoologist. A site which is important from different points of view should be studied in full collaboration. In such an approach there is recognition of archaeology as being not merely scientific, but a science.

VI-THE ARCHAEOLOGIST AS ARTIST AND CRAFTSMAN

ANCIENT MAN PROBABLY HAD NO WORD TO SIGNIFY THE CONCEPT of art. He made his stone axes and bronze daggers as well as he could and never thought of skimping on workmanship to increase production. He decorated his creations to satisfy some vague craving in his own soul, to insure good luck in hunting or in battle, or to please the many gods he feared and prayed to. At times he used a decorative pattern simply out of respect for tradition.

Primitive man therefore knew no artists as distinct from craftsmen. And the modern archaeologist likewise makes no distinction. He may admire cave paintings of twenty thousand years ago, but if another archaeologist or an artist disagrees with him about their aesthetic value, the disagreement is primarily a matter of personal taste and not of archaeology. The archaeologist is not an art critic, and the appreciation of beauty is not his main business. He is most interested in the nature of the objects painted, the truthfulness of the reflection of primitive life, the meaning of the painting for the painter, and the techniques by which the work was accomplished. Scholars may marvel at the pottery and feathered robes created by the ancient peoples of Peru or at the filigree work of Egyptian craftsmen, but as students of technical skill rather than as critics of artistic values.

Every object created by man requires skill for its making. The archaeologist must therefore be a student of all skills and of their development. He must be interested in the full range of human activities from music and prize-fighting to how-to-do-it yourself. Each of these has its history and its prehistory, and it is the archaeologist's business to trace them.

This difficult task he accomplishes by the study of material remains. The objects that people left behind them offer a double challenge: the unraveling of both the purpose for which they were used and of the manner in which they were made. If he can accomplish these two feats he has gone a long way toward understanding the culture they represent.

He begins his study therefore with the very earliest artifacts that Paleolithic Man left behind—flaked stones. What kinds of stone did the early hunters seek, where did they find the flints and pieces of obsidian they prized, how did they learn to chip them into useful objects? What shapes did these objects take? Were they used as axheads, chipping tools, or gouging tools?

With all the training that modern man's brain has undergone in the half million or so years since the Old Stone Age, or Paleolithic Era, began, the proper way to flake a flint is still not easily determined. Archaeologists who try to reproduce Stone Age weapons cannot bang one stone against another and get a usable blade. They have been forced to learn by trial and error what type of object to use for striking, how and where to hit the stone being shaped, and so on. Learning all these things has not taken them the hundred thousand years or so it took primitive man. But it has required much thought and considerable experiment.

Primitive people learned very early to make fire and to cook their food. But after a time the domestic arts, which included brewing, were left mostly to women. The male's job was to hunt and fish; the female's job was to take care of her children and the needs of the nomadic household. She gathered nuts and seeds, made the baskets in which they were collected, and learned how to store and preserve them. When clothing a family became more complicated than stripping the skin from a slain animal, she apparently invented the spinning and weaving of cloth. Among some primitive tribes of the present day the making of pottery is also part of woman's work, and this appears to have been true in prehistoric days as well. When the potter's wheel was invented, however, and pottery-making became a full-time profession, it fell into the hands of men. In those days women who faced the now traditional conflict of family versus career had no choice. Families were thrust upon them, careers taken away. It should be remembered that there were primitive societies, however, in which the roles of men and women were somewhat reversed.

By the time man entered the New Stone Age, or the Neolithic Age, his craftsmanship was highly developed. He was a skilled worker not only in stone but in bone, antler, wood, and ivory as well. A hunter, trapper, and fisher of great experience, he had invented throwing sticks, spears, javelins, bows and arrows, harpoons, blowguns, the lasso and other forms of noose, fishing lines and hooks, traps and nets—all in a tremendous variety of forms. He barbed his hooks, harpoons, and arrows to make sure they would not come loose, and tipped his darts with poisons. He had also become a practical zoologist, acquainted with the habits of reindeer, wild pigs, and different kinds of fish.

He learned how to supply his houses with doors, chairs, and tables. Most of his wooden furniture, naturally, has decayed

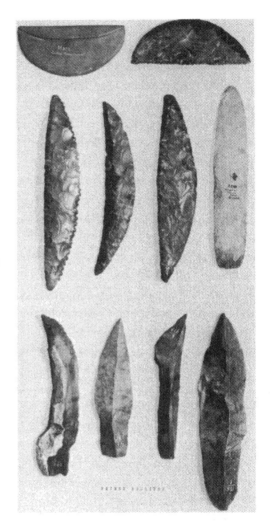

Implements of the recent
Neolithic Age

or been destroyed by worms and insects. Occasionally, however, as in the Neolithic village of Skara Brae, in the Orkney
Islands, he constructed his beds, dressers, and other furniture
not of wood but of stone slabs, and in this case we can get
an idea of what he considered comfortable living.

[66]

Neolithic Man was a home owner, and primarily a farmer. By this time man had progressed from simple food-gathering to food production. Having tamed his animals and domesticated a large number of plants, he developed yokes for his beasts of burden and fences for them and his food animals. He discovered that the growing of plants was not simply a matter of scattering seed on the ground, but a complicated process of choosing his soil carefully, ploughing the ground either by the strength of his muscles or those of his oxen, sowing his crops at the proper time, and supplying enough water, by irrigation if need be.

Rectangular house of the Neolithic period at County Limerick

He had also become a miner, not at first for the metals which would soon assume so much importance in his life, but for the proper kinds of stone. A study of some of the flint mines he worked shows that he recognized the need for proper drainage and ventilation in his mining shafts.

His methods of transportation were still primitive. The wheeled cart did not come into use until the beginning of the Bronze Age, but Neolithic Man did utilize various forms of sledges. And Neolithic Woman had learned to spin threads of flax, wool, or cotton, to weave fabrics of them, and to fashion the fabrics into clothes.

When man entered the Bronze Age he gained many new skills and lost a few of the old ones. Hunting and fishing became of less importance to him, and some of his ability to make traps, nets, harpoons, and other instruments for the capture or slaughter of wild life disappeared. But his skill in killing his fellow man increased. The use of bronze made it possible to fashion better swords and daggers, as well as improved helmets and shields. From the occasional conflict of tribe with tribe, Bronze Age Man developed the art of war, and invented special gods to pray to for his enemy's death.

He perfected the mining of copper and tin, the metals from which bronze was made. Even in those days mining was a dirty, unpleasant, and dangerous job, customarily reserved for criminals, slaves, and prisoners of war. Another occupation for the unfortunate was quarrying. The Egyptians learned to cut and move granite or limestone blocks weighing hundreds of tons, and most of the cutting and moving had to be done by human muscles. But the human brain did supply some aid. Instruments had been invented for splitting and chiseling stone, and skilled foremen could avoid cracking the blocks they wanted to cut.

Bronze tools made possible the easier handling of wood or

granite by carpenter or stone mason, as well as the careful, detailed work of the cabinet maker, jeweler, engraver, goldsmith, and silversmith. Bronze Age Man learned to solder and weld metal, to produce fine filigree work, to use inlays and enamel on metal, to combine gold and ivory and precious stones. Such work required a rare combination of skill, patience, and knowledge of materials, and some of the masterpieces of ancient Egypt or Mesopotamia have never been surpassed.

The Bronze Age saw the invention of the wheeled cart and chariot, the improvement from solid to spoked wheels, the extension of irrigation canals into complicated systems, the building of bridges, and the evolution of rafts and dugout canoes into seagoing sailing vessels capable of making long voyages. Improved methods for the dyeing of textiles and the tanning of leather, as well as the creation of glass and the invention of methods of embalming, all testified to man's increasing knowledge of practical chemistry.

Bronze Age Man studied the stars and learned to predict eclipses and phases of the moon. He worked out a system of weights and measures and devised a number of ways of telling time. Now he no longer built a hut meant to last a few days or seasons. He became a splendid architect, and created palaces and temples to outlast the ages.

Thanks to the improvement of methods of farming, he had reached the point where he could afford temples and palaces. Farmers could feed not only themselves and their families, but the architects, stone-cutters, builders, and other artisans, so that it became possible to build cities whose inhabitants did not themselves produce food. It was the needs of city life that led to more complicated social and political developments, as well as to the growth of mathematics and the development of writing.

In all these activities Bronze Age Man was both craftsman

and artist, and in both aspects he interests the archaeologist. Here and there some ancient technique has been lost. But for the most part archaeologists have learned how he created his wonders, whether they were Egyptian pyramids or the fine feather robes of the Peruvian Indians.

The archaeologist's relation to the arts and crafts is thus different from his relation to the sciences. The latter are of the present and can help him in his investigations. But the arts and crafts in which he is most interested belong to the past. They comprise the material aspects of ancient life, and he cannot understand that life without knowing a great deal about them.

To put it simply, the archaeologist is asked to know everything about anything that interested his predecessors. We shall soon see how he has put to good use a great deal of apparently useless information.

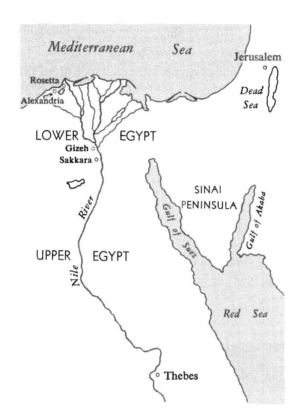

VII - MUMMIES LIVE AGAIN

Ancient Egypt, unlike Pompeii, has never been forgotten. The Bible has painted so vivid a picture of the oppression of the Children of Israel in the land of Egypt that the word "Pharaoh" has become a synonym for a cruel tyrant. It was the Pharaohs who ordered the building of the stupendous pyramids, so they could be certain of a resting place for their souls. These are great heaps of stone of which the most famous was constructed almost five thousand years ago by Khufu (known to the Greeks as Cheops) near what is now Cairo. This great pyramid, which originally rose to a height of more than four hundred and eighty feet, has shrunk thirty feet in its centuries of existence, but it still contains more than two million stone blocks, each weighing about two and a half tons. According to Herodotus, its construction required the work of a hundred thousand men for twenty years. Also, it required the planning of a great architect.

About eighty pyramids are known, most of them constructed within an interval of little more than five hundred years, from 2815 to 2294 B.C. Almost as impressive as any pyramid is the Great Sphinx at Gizeh, a creature with the head of a man and the body of a lion, two hundred and fifty

Aerial view of the Sphinx

feet long and sixty-six feet high. It is the largest of many sphinxes constructed to guard temples and tombs.

These massive memorials of architecture and engineering never ceased to arouse the wonder of the ancient world. Standing in seemingly untouched splendor amid the shifting sands of the desert, existing apparently from the beginning of time and destined to exist till its end, the pyramids had become symbols of Eternity even two thousand years ago, in the time of Cleopatra, last queen of ancient Egypt.

The Romans, who conquered Egypt, also helped keep alive the memory of ancient glories. Like other conquerors, they carried away to their own land whatever they could lay their hands on. They even removed granite obelisks, tall columns which weighed several hundred tons each, and which provided difficult problems in naval transportation. Once in Rome, the obelisks added little enough to a knowledge of Egyptian culture. But they were a constant reminder that a great civilization had existed south of the Mediterranean.

Unfortunately, they did not keep alive the knowledge of that civilization's language. From about 3200 B.C. on, when its written history begins, Egypt had used three forms of writing. The earliest, known to the Greeks and hence to us as *hieroglyphics,* or sacred carvings (because of their use by the priests), consisted of pictures chiseled on stone. In addition to the symbols for words, hieroglyphics also used symbols for syllables or sounds. Later the Egyptians began to write on *papyrus,* an early paper made from reeds which grew along the Nile. For writing on papyrus the priests modified hieroglyphics into a form called *hieratic,* and this was further simplified later into a script called *demotic.* The symbols could be written more quickly, and hence were more useful for commercial transactions and other worldly pursuits.

From their first use to the time when their meaning was forgotten, the three forms of writing spanned thirty-five hundred years of Egyptian history. Exactly how and why the memory of the old script died out we do not know. There must have been many factors, from the coming into use of the superior Greek and Latin alphabets to the dying out of the old civilization, along with the decline of the Egyptian priesthood. In addition, the subjugation of Egypt to one foreign conqueror after another must also have played a part. Whatever the most important causes, more than fifteen hundred years ago the ancient hieroglyphic, hieratic, and demotic scripts did fall into disuse, along with the spoken language itself, and both the mummies and the gods of ancient Egypt slumbered in their graves, waiting for some one capable of bringing them to life.

The rediscovery of Pompeii, early in the eighteenth century, led to the rediscovery of the entire ancient world. Interest in Egypt soon revived, but a knowledge of hieroglyphics of course did not. A language cannot be dug up as a city can. For a century or more some scholars even doubted that the hieroglyphics *were* a form of writing. They seemed like mere stylized curlicues, ornamenting statues and monuments.

The first great advance in the modern archaeological study of Egypt was an indirect result of the French revolution. In 1798, a few years before Napoleon became Emperor of France, he sailed to conquer northeast Africa. He took along with him, in addition to his soldiers, almost two hundred scientists and scholars. While the soldiers fought, the scientists had a busy and enjoyable time, collecting an enormous number of specimens, statues, and carved stones. The pyramids were too heavy to be moved, but the French scholars followed the tradition of all conquerors in liberating whatever they could.

Toward the end of 1798, the British under Admiral Nelson cornered the French fleet near the mouth of the Nile and smashed it completely. Napoleon, aware even before the term had been invented that common soldiers were expendable, whereas a man of his greatness must be preserved for posterity, deserted his army and slipped back to Europe in a small ship. The scientists, like the soldiers, were left to find their way back as best they could. Also left behind were several artists, who copied inscriptions from pyramids or obelisks, and made plaster casts.

The great Egyptian expedition had apparently come to an end, both from the military and the scientific points of view. Then, in 1799, several of Napoleon's expendable soldiers made a sensational discovery. This was a tablet of black stone, about four feet by two and a half in surface dimensions, and almost a foot thick. This Rosetta Stone, as it came to be known, contained that hoped for and unexpected miracle—a magic key to the writings of ancient Egypt. Inscribed on it in three parallel columns were Egyptian hieroglyphics, Egyptian demotic, and ancient Greek. Obviously, the same message had been inscribed in the three forms of writing. Translate one, thought the eager scholars, and you translated all.

So they translated one, the ancient Greek, which they knew well. They found this to be a decree in honor of King Ptolemy V, dated 196 B.C. They thereupon turned eagerly to hieroglyphics and demotic, and discovered that the Greek inscription did not help them much in translating the Egyptian scripts.

At this point political events interfered with scientific studies. With the British now masters of the Mediterranean, it was clear that Egypt too would soon fall completely into their hands, and with it the treasures that the French scholars had found. A plaster cast was therefore made of the Rosetta

The Rosetta Stone. The upper inscription is hieroglyphic, the middle one Demotic, and the bottom, Greek.

Stone and other valuable objects too large to be concealed. Later, when the Stone itself was surrendered, to be installed in sedate triumph in the British Museum, the French had their copy, just as they had copies of thousands of other inscriptions. For hieroglyphic and demotic scripts had been discovered everywhere in Egypt, on obelisks and monuments, on broken pieces of stone and clay pillars, and on rolls of papyrus. Of all these thousands of inscriptions, it was still impossible to translate a word.

Scholars returned to their study of the Rosetta Stone. But the great hopes of immediate success had by now been dashed. They might know the general meaning of a long series of strange marks, but how could they find the specific meaning of every individual sign among the thousands which represented a language unspoken for fifteen centuries? Any one who has tried to translate the writings of a Greek or Latin poet with the help of a dictionary and a grammar, some training in the poet's language, and possibly a "pony" to help, has learned that, even under these circumstances, it may be difficult to understand the poet's meaning. How could the scholars even begin to translate, knowing not one letter, not one word, not a single fact about verbs or nouns or pronouns?

Despite all difficulties, a modest beginning was made by the British scholar Thomas Young. Young had discovered the Egyptian symbols for the name *Ptolemy*. A modest beginning indeed! For of the thousands of signs, these letters represented only a tiny fraction. Which symbols stood for words, which for syllables? Was their meaning changed when they were put together in different ways? Young went on working at such problems, but his progress was slow.

A brilliant young Frenchman, Jean François Champollion, took up the challenge of the Rosetta Stone shortly after Young. Champollion had prepared himself for the task by learning as much about Egypt as he could, and by mastering a number of ancient and modern Oriental tongues, including Coptic, spoken by some modern Egyptians. Coptic was considerably different from ancient Egyptian. But Champollion expected to find in the modern language at least traces of the ancient, and he hoped that the modern language, both in words and in sentence structure, might give him clues to its long-dead predecessor. As it turned out, he was right.

First he confirmed the fact that Young was correct in his interpretation of the name *Ptolemy*. In the Greek he found another name, that of Cleopatra, and went on to decipher it in hieroglyphics. With a few more letters at his disposal, he was now able to pick up a syllable here, a word there. Checking the meaning of each new sign against the other inscriptions available, he slowly and laboriously worked out the meaning of one after another. By 1822, after years of this slow and tedious process of inspired guessing and careful checking, he succeeded in deciphering the entire hieroglyphic inscription.

Other symbols were yet to be encountered, and some of Champollion's translation would have to be revised. But taken as a whole, his accomplishment is a splendid triumph of the human intellect, and with it the back of the problem was broken. It was now possible to construct a grammar and dictionary of the ancient Egyptian language, and as scholars became familiar with it, they began to translate one after another of the numerous inscriptions that had baffled them through the years.

With Champollion's great achievement to spur them on, the students of Egyptian antiquity became more active than ever. The land was covered with tombs and with the remains of its ancient inhabitants. The dryness of air and soil helped preserve for generations not only the bones but even the bodies of mummies and unmummified Egyptians alike. Rolls of papyrus which in any other country would long since have crumbled into dust here remained beautifully preserved thousands of years after they were written. And objects of gold or precious stones lasted for endless centuries, becoming ever more valuable with the passage of time.

Egypt soon swarmed with fortune hunters. Adventurers, peasants, and scholars ransacked the country in hit or miss fashion, with or without a scientific basis upon which to work. The best-known pyramids and tombs were the first to be attacked. But people dug everywhere, for there was hardly a spot in ancient Egypt that could not become the scene of a great find. Soon it became impossible to tell adventurer from scholar. Both individuals were often combined in the same person, for scholars used bribery, robbery, and armed force whenever they had to, and the most successful adventurers became scholars in order to learn what loot it best paid to steal.

The most famous of these adventurers was Giovanni Belzoni (1778-1823), a former strong man on the London music-hall stage. In 1815, while Champollion was still struggling with the riddle of the Rosetta Stone, Belzoni went to Egypt to sell a water wheel he had invented. He stayed to become a collector of antiquities, small and large. In the tradition of his Roman ancestors, he even collected obelisks, for which there was a good market in Europe.

In Belzoni's day, however, collecting had its dangers. On one occasion he was peacefully going his way with one of these several-hundred-ton treasures when he encountered two other antiquarians of the same sort as himself. These other gentlemen had the advantage of pistols and rifles, and attempted to take his obelisk away from him. Apparently they failed. The incident is strongly reminiscent of a train robbery in a Western movie.

Like the strong man he was when not confronted with

Temple to the Gods. Luxor Temple is one of the most impressive sights of contemporary Luxor, 420 miles south of Cairo, as it was when "Hundred-gated" Thebes was the capital of Egypt 4,000 years ago.

firearms, Belzoni opened tombs by strong-arm methods, smashing them with battering rams, crushing mummies, skeletons, and tomb furniture, and ripping away whatever he could use. He was, however, no worse than other collectors and so-called archaeologists of his time. And he did set later scholars on the trail of important discoveries. He found several tombs of Pharaohs, among them one in what is known as the Valley of the Kings, near Thebes. Later investigators showed the soil of this same valley to be fertile in other great discoveries.

About twenty years after Belzoni's death in 1823, Auguste

Mariette arrived in Cairo from France to buy manuscripts for the Louvre museum. Mariette was horrified by the plundering of Egyptian antiquities he saw around him, as well as by the senseless destruction of ancient treasures, and determined to stop the indiscriminate looting. Eventually he was to have some success in this laudable endeavor. Meanwhile, he himself did a tremendous amount of excavation. Seeking great finds—and there were still many of these in Egypt—he made such imposing discoveries as the Alley of the Sphinxes at Sakkara, a town near Cairo. In this region he discovered a hundred and forty sphinxes. Elsewhere he uncovered tombs and temples, using some of the prevailing archaeological techniques of his day. How advanced these were can be seen from his use of dynamite to blast away the ruins of a temple which interfered with his digging.

And yet, despite the dynamiting and other forms of destruction for which Mariette was responsible, he did contribute greatly to the rising science of Egyptology, that branch of archaeology concerned with Egyptian antiquity. Becoming Director of the Egyptian Service of Antiquities, he reserved to himself all rights to excavate, and thus temporarily stopped looting by collectors and tomb robbers. He fought to establish a Museum of Egyptian Antiquities, and helped end the export to Europe of valuable archaeological finds. Like Belzoni, Mariette had clashes with bands of robbers, but with the government to support him he usually came out ahead, saving many treasures for his museum.

Despite the fact that Mariette's chief interest lay in the discovery of grand and imposing monuments and rich collections of jewels, he helped paint an interesting and detailed picture of ancient life. So far Egyptology had been concerned almost entirely with the activities of kings and nobles. But

among Mariette's finds were tomb decorations showing how
the ordinary Egyptians prepared flax, cut trees, and went about
their other daily tasks. He helped make the entire pattern of
Egyptian society glow with vivid color.

The first genuinely modern excavator in Egypt was William
Matthew Flinders Petrie. Born in 1853, Petrie was sickly from
birth, suffered from asthmatic attacks—and lived a busy and
adventurous life to the ripe age of eighty-nine. Petrie must
have chosen his life's work almost from the cradle, for he took
seriously the archaeologist's need to know many languages, and
at the age of eight was already studying French, Latin, and
Greek, in addition to English. These and other studies, however, were too much for his feeble health, and a collapse soon
put an end to all formal education.

But as far as his health permitted, he continued studying
on his own. An interest in surveying led him to emphasize the
need for careful measurement. He realized the importance of
details, and turned the attention of Eyptologists to the small
and unimpressive objects they had neglected—the undecorated
pottery which seemed to have little artistic value and was not
wanted by museums, the ugly and corroded tools, broken
fragments of all kinds. In these objects lay some of the most
important evidence sought by archaeologists.

When Petrie began his work in Egyptology, he encountered
ignorance on all sides, not only of correct methods of excavation, of taking notes, and of the need for full publication of
discoveries, but of how to preserve what was excavated. Museum officials let the treasures in their care deteriorate, and in
some cases ruined the value of collections by indiscriminate
trading. They did not realize that an object had archaeological
value only when its relations with other objects found with
it were known.

A tomb of the First Dynasty (about 3000 B.C.) at Saqqara, Egypt. Careful measurements of the subterranean burial chamber are being made by Egyptian workman for the architect and chief of the expedition.

Petrie had both the skill and the dedication of the true scientist. In 1880 he began work on the three pyramids of Gizeh. For two years he made his home in a tomb near the pyramids—not the actual burial place itself, but an upper chamber where the ancient Egyptians had left offerings for the mummified body. Here, in a room cut out of the solid rock, its temperature almost unchanging, he lived with his kerosene cookstove. Waiting until the sun had set and the gaping tourists had left, he would strip naked and with his notebook and lamp enter a pyramid.

Inside the vast heap of stone the air was hot and close. Every movement he made stirred a cloud of fine dust which after several hours produced fever and headache. Petrie's asthma made him sensitive to dust of all kinds, and soon every breath was torture. But not until after midnight did he stumble out of the pyramid again, his lungs straining for air, his body streaming with sweat which sometimes stained his notebook. He went through corridor after corridor of the pyramids, making careful measurements that no one before him had thought of making. During the daylight hours he also made a complete survey of the area around the three pyramids, taking careful measurements which he repeated again and again. By the time his first season was over, he knew most of the distances between important points within a quarter of an inch or less.

Surveying, excavating, making measurements inside the pyramids, and writing up his notes, completely filled his time. In addition to the dangers of dust and heat there were other, more sudden and dramatic, perils. Once, just as he came out of a pit, he was almost buried by a shower of stones. And working alone, as he usually did, there was always the chance that if he found anything of value he would be attacked by thieves, robbed, and murdered.

Nevertheless he worked happily and fruitfully, and when he had completed his work at Gizeh, the world had a picture of the pyramids that surpassed in accuracy any previously made.

Later on Petrie dug in many places in Egypt, working at Abydos, in the Delta, and in the Valley of the Kings on the west bank of the Nile. He made a number of important contributions to the growing science of Egyptology, from methods for the preservation of objects found to a new technique called *sequence dating*. At a time when absolute dates were unknown and the archaeological record could not yet be correlated with inscriptions and historical reports, dates could be determined only relatively, chiefly by types of pottery. Petrie arbitrarily divided the history of Egypt into fifty sequence dates, from period 30 to period 79. The periods from 20 to 29 were assigned to prehistoric Egypt. Each period was defined only by types, not by number of years. The number of years might differ greatly from period to period, but it was possible by Petrie's method to distinguish early events from late ones, and as absolute dates were found, to assign an approximate number of years to each period. First developed for Egypt, this method was later applied all over the world, and has been found useful in American archaeology as well as in the Old World.

The Valley of the Kings was not the site of any of Petrie's more famous excavations. Nevertheless, he was interested here, as other Egyptologists had been, in the records of excavators whose digging had long preceded his. These were tomb robbers, no mere gang of minor criminals, but a network of priests, politicians, and officials in the government itself.

Most of the robberies occurred shortly after burial of a king or queen. One of the local priests, a worker on a tomb, or a participant in the funeral ceremony might, in exchange for a share of the loot, inform the robbers of the location of the tomb. Across the Nile from Thebes, the City of the Dead was regularly looted—and then it was discovered that the mayor of Western Thebes and his entire administration formed part of the robber gang. A crooked mayor working with gangsters is an unexpectedly modern touch to the story of ancient Egypt. And there is another modern touch—the fact that the commission appointed to investigate the crime exonerated the mayor and found his accuser guilty. Later it was found that some of the commissioners were themselves linked with the thieves! Eventually the thieves were condemned, tortured, and executed. Soon after, however, other grave robbers took their place.

Under the Egyptian system, grave robbery was inevitable. The people wanted their gods—the Pharaohs—to live on among the things they had been accustomed to in life, so they made sure that the gold and jewels they had owned during life were buried along with their mummies. These treasures were so numerous and of such great value that nothing could protect them. The very people appointed to guard them turned into thieves.

There were few unbelievers in ancient Egypt. Everyone was convinced of the power of the gods, everyone knew that the mummies of the king and queen were under the protection of such powerful deities as Isis and Osiris, as well as Horus, son of the divine couple. One of these three would inevitably lay a curse upon any violator of the tombs. Yet the thought of this curse was no deterrent. Thieves by the thousand risked the displeasure of the gods, made a profession of grave-robbing, and lived happily, if guiltily, ever after.

Petrie's careful work was a lesson to all later investigators. In some respects, excavation in Egypt had been too simple, and archaeologists inexperienced in work in other countries did not know how to face difficulties. Pyramids and sphinxes were easy to recognize, and so were rock tombs and walls buried in sand. But what happened when excavators dug through mud along the Nile, and encountered the damp remains of ancient structures made of mud brick? Very often they could not recognize the softened brick at all, and dug it away along with the other mud.

Close attention to detail was needed—an eye for faint differences of color, for every trace of ancient artifacts. Petrie's attention to trifles paid off in one brilliant discovery of great importance. In 1889 and 1890 he uncovered at Egyptian sites remains of different dynasties, along with some hitherto unknown pottery. The unknown pottery was of early Greek type, and Petrie guessed that it was from Mycenae and Crete, from very early Greek civilizations. He was in this way able to match Greek dates against Egyptian. The early Greek or Aegean civilization was dated at 2500 B.C., the Mycenaean from 1500 to 1000 B.C.

It is one of the ironies of archaeology that possibly the most important single discovery during this period was made not by a famous archaeologist but by an Egyptian peasant woman who in 1887 found at Tell el Amarna, site of the royal city of Amenhotep IV, or Akhnaton, tablets of baked clay covered with symbols of a type used by the Sumerians and Babylonians in Asia. Her find was at first neglected. When at last some attention was paid to it, the experts asked sharp questions. What was an Asian script doing in Egypt? They suspected that some dealer with an eye for the sensational was trying to put over a clever forgery.

After a time, however, as no one seemed anxious to profit by the forgeries, the experts took a second look and discovered

that the tablets consisted of the diplomatic correspondence between Egypt and other kingdoms during the fourteenth century B.C. The tablets were published by German archaeologists,
and the site was studied by a number of others, including
Petrie. In all, three hundred letters were found between Egypt
and Babylon, Assyria, the Hittites, the Phoenicians, and especially the Syrians. The correspondence proved to be a treasure
house of information about Egyptian and Asiatic affairs.

Egyptology was slowly becoming more scientific, and
methods of digging were improving. But brilliant guesses, inspiration, and plain luck continued to play a part. The Valley
of the Kings had been a favorite site for excavation from the
time of Belzoni on, and it is amusing to note that over a
period of a century each man who dug there and made an
important discovery convinced himself that he had found all
that was left to find.

By 1917, however, it really did seem as if nothing of importance were left. A good part of the Valley had already been
dug up by archaeologists, not to mention the ever-present tomb
robbers. But the young British archaeologist Howard Carter
felt that an important find was still to be made. With the aid
and support of the Earl of Carnarvon he set out to make the
greatest discovery of all. Carter had observed among the finds
of the American Theodore Davis a cup bearing the name of
Tutankhamen, son-in-law of Akhnaton. Davis had also found
in a small tomb a wooden box bearing the same name, and
concluded that the tomb was Tutankhamen's. Carter did not
think so. He felt that the tomb of Tutankhamen was yet to be
uncovered in this same Valley of Kings.

Carter's reasoning was excellent. His luck was not quite so
good. True, he picked a hopeful site for excavation and in the
first season's work came across workmen's huts which indi-

The golden mask of King Tutankhamen, now in the Museum of Egyptian Antiquities.

cated the presence of a tomb nearby. But during the next few seasons his hopes were aroused only to be disappointed. In the autumn of 1922 he made a decision to spend one last season excavating in the Valley, in the area where he had first come across the huts.

Now his luck appeared to have changed. No sooner were the huts cleared away than steps appeared, cut in the stone underneath. Soon it became clear that they led to the entrance of a tomb, a sealed doorway. Carter sent a telegram to Lord Carnarvon and waited impatiently for the other man's arrival. Two and a half weeks later the door was cleared.

Examination showed that the tomb had been opened and closed twice. Robbers had in fact entered it. But the fact that it had been sealed again showed that they had not plundered the tomb completely.

[89]

The door was opened, and a passage filled with stone was cleared away. Now a second door stood revealed. This too was opened, and inside Carter found two magnificent black statues, along with golden objects. Here too was evidence of the instrusion of thieves. But the presence of so many objects showed that the thieves had been frightened or driven away before they could complete their looting. Moreover, there was neither a sarcophagus nor a mummy.

Carter did discover another sealed door. Eager as he was to uncover the treasures that lay beyond it, however, he and Carnarvon paused. Already they had found, in the chamber with the two statues and in an annex to it, a tremendous number of articles of great archaeological value. It would take months and possibly years to study them. If they were to find the burial chamber intact, they would need to be extremely careful to prevent many of the objects from falling apart. There must be thorough preparation.

Carter resealed the tomb, posted a guard, and prepared to preserve, pack, and catalogue what he had found and hoped to find. By now the discovery had been announced to the world, and offers of help arrived from archaeologists everywhere. When the tomb was reopened, work was begun on the antechamber, and the seal of the inner door was slowly loosened.

Inside was a golden shrine and additional treasure. But the opening of the shrine had to wait. Lord Carnarvon died, and there were difficulties with the Egyptian Government. It was not until 1928 that the mummy of Tutankhamen was finally reached. To Carter's delight, it was untouched by thieves.

Tutankhamen's was the only royal tomb thus far found that had escaped plundering. Thieves had indeed invaded it, but had been driven off. Never before had such treasures of every kind been discovered in a Pharaoh's burial place. Tutankhamen himself was of little importance, and if he had not been Akhnaton's brother-in-law would probably never have become Pharaoh. He had died at eighteen, with no great accomplishment to his credit except his accession to the throne, and only the fortunate preservation of his tomb, and Carter's brilliant work in finding it, has made him important to archaeologists.

The mass of Egyptian material now accumulated in museums will take dozens of years to study, and some archaeologists feel that so much is now known about the Egyptian dynasties that further work cannot add any fundamentally new results. They feel that now there is nothing to do in this field but fill in the details.

Other archaeologists and scholars disagree. It is true, however, that the history of Egypt from about 3200 B.C. on, thanks chiefly to archaeological research, is, in general, now known. Prior to that year the country had been divided into two kingdoms, Upper Egypt (in the South, below the Delta) and Lower Egypt (in the North). In 3200 B.C. the two kingdoms were united under Menes, first king of the First Dynasty. From then on we have a continuous, if incomplete, story of what happened. We know that the country was invaded several times, fought many wars, and passed through periods of prosperity and hardship. There were civil strife and war against other kingdoms. Kings struggled for the throne, priests fought each other for the primacy of their different gods, and at one period, from 1377 to 1360 B.C., the Pharaoh Akhnaton, or Amenhotep IV, replaced the old Egyptian belief in many gods with a religion in which only a single god was worshipped. Akhnaton's reign was brief and his reforms did not outlast his death. But they form a curious episode in ancient history, whose significance in the history of religion has been much debated.

Archaeology has also revealed much of the daily life of the Egyptian common people. For every king and queen there were of course millions of peasants and other ordinary Egyptians who never enjoyed the luxury of burial in great tombs. Thanks to the attention such men as Petrie paid to apparently trivial finds, we have learned about the houses in which they lived, the food they ate, the objects they created in stone and glass and metal, the skills they acquired in carpentry and leatherwork and jewelry, the sufferings they underwent, and the diseases which killed them. It is now possible to read about these things in the hieroglyphics of ancient monuments, to see them in tomb illustrations, to deduce them from fragments of artifacts and mummies.

Meanwhile, much more attention is now being paid to the early days of Egypt, before the First Dynasty, before the use of hieroglyphics for writing, before the building of pyramids and sphinxes. Study of this period is necessary in order to answer the question of how Egyptian civilization arose. Did the Egyptians create their own writing or borrow the idea from the Sumerians? Did they develop civilization by their own efforts or did these same Sumerians set the example?

It is the great unanswered questions that most attract archaeologists. If the attraction is great enough, they may not remain long unanswered.

VIII=BEFORE THE BIBLE

THE BIBLE, ESPECIALLY THE OLD TESTAMENT, HAS BEEN A wonderful source of clues for archaeologists. The very features of the original Greek or Hebrew text which sometimes make translators rack their brains for years have often repaid the closest study. Passages which at first sight seem purely poetic imagery often turn out to be descriptions of customs or ways of life long forgotten. And Biblical listings of long-dead peoples and kingdoms, which most readers tend to skip, are capsules of ancient history which reveal on careful analysis their tales of war and conquest.

The Biblical events are described as occurring in Mesopo-tamia and to a lesser extent in Egypt, the two areas where civilization took its first steps from the cradle. That the story of Adam and Eve should have been set by ancient authors in the valley of the Tigris-Euphrates rivers—Mesopotamia means "between the rivers"—can hardly be pure coincidence.

Of course it is no coincidence to those who believe literally in the Biblical book of Genesis and locate the Garden of Eden in this same valley. Archaeologists, however, are not literal believers in any event unsupported by evidence based on excavation, and the tale of Adam and Eve and the serpent therefore finds them skeptical. But the occurrence of other, more probable events, either directly reported or implied by the writers of the Bible, has been repeatedly confirmed.

Our knowledge of the Assyrians and Babylonians and of their history, for example, was for many centuries based on accounts in Herodotus and a few other Greek writers and on the Old Testament. The Hebrew prophets had long denounced the wicked luxury of the Babylonians and the ferocity of the Assyrians. But the full extent to which these denunciations were deserved was not suspected until serious archaeological excavations began, with Biblical references to guide and inspire the digging.

The prophets, naturally, had never reported the high level of culture attained by the ancient inhabitants of Mesopotamia, nor for that matter had the Greek historians. To the prophets most of their enemies were doomed to destruction as idolators, while to the Greeks, most Asians, prophets included, were individuals who did not appreciate the finer things of life, and lacked knowledge of important philosophical matters. Herodotus, for example, was more impressed by the physical greatness of Babylon than by its culture.

In the seventeenth century the ground was laid for a change of opinion. Business men, adventurers, and pleasure seekers from England and Continental Europe began to travel through eastern Asia, and it became fashionable to pick up odd souvenirs and to note strange features of ancient monuments. In 1808, Claudius James Rich, appointed British resident in Baghdad, became what might be called the first roving archaeologist in Mesopotamia. He visited the sites of ruined cities and collected manuscripts, jewelry, and a number of remarkable tablets which he brought back to England to arouse the curiosity of the British public.

Rich, like the other collectors of his time, had only a vague idea of the significance of his treasures. Among the objects which puzzled scholars as early as the seventeenth century were copies of inscriptions in *cuneiform* or wedge-shaped characters. The same characters appeared on Rich's tablets. For more than a century before his time, experts had debated whether these weird-looking symbols were actually a form of writing or mere ornamental decoration.

This same argument had raged about Egyptian hieroglyphics, and for a similar reason. The glory that was Greece and the grandeur that was Rome, long before their own collapse, had destroyed the more ancient glories and grandeurs of Babylon and Egypt. Just as Caesar's conquest of Egypt led to the displacement of different Egyptian scripts by the Roman and Greek alphabets, so Alexander's conquest of Persia led gradually to the displacement of cuneiform writing, and resulted eventually in the very nature of cuneiform symbols being forgotten for twenty centuries.

What time had destroyed, scientific curiosity helped to revive. As more and more examples of cuneiform were discovered, it became clear that they *must* be forms of writing and not mere ornaments. This was true even before the discovery of the famous inscriptions at Persepolis and Behistun

in what was once the ancient empire of Persia, but the inscriptions settled the question once and for all. In both places
cuneiform writing occurred in three columns which apparently
said the same thing in different languages. The middle inscriptions, occupying the most important place, were most
likely in Persian—the language of the rulers. But that question could be settled definitely only when they were translated. The columns at Behistun were longer and therefore
more valuable to would-be translators, but unfortunately they
were inscribed high up on the side of a sheer and almost
inaccessible cliff.

Nevertheless, to George Friedrich Grotefend (1775-1853), a
German teacher, the inscriptions at Persepolis were enough for
a start. Reasoning as Champollion had done that when a king
recorded an event his most passionate interest was the glorifi-
cation of his own name, Grotefend began about 1800 to scan
cuneiform inscriptions for the set formula with which Persian
kings introduced themselves to posterity. As was known from
other sources, this was "X, great King, King of Kings, King
of A and B, son of Y," etc. He was able to detect a significant
omission. King Y announced himself as "Great King, King of
Kings, son of Z," but after Z there was no word for King. X
was King; his father, Y, was also King; but Grandfather Z
was not a King at all. From what was known of Persian history, it soon became clear that Z was Hystaspes, while X and
Y were Xerxes and Darius respectively. Grotefend was able
to pick out the signs for these three names, the symbols for
king and son, and a few others as well. Scholars who followed
in his trail began with great difficulty to compile a cuneiform
dictionary.

But without the long inscriptions on the cliffs at Behistun
the work went slowly. This was a problem that called for a

combination of scholarly devotion and the courage and reckless daring of a young man.

As so often happens, the problem seemed to evoke the existence of a man to solve it. Henry Rawlinson, a young British army officer, had both a passionate interest in tackling the scientific puzzle and the physical courage to challenge the cliffs. As Champollion had learned Coptic in order to translate ancient Egyptian, Rawlinson mastered Parsi, a language descended from ancient Persian. Without it he would have been helpless before the Behistun inscriptions. Unaware of Grotefend's work, he too worked out the names of the three Persian kings. In 1835, deciding that he could no longer do without the Behistun inscriptions, he climbed the cliffs several times a day and set to work to copy, sign by sign, the Persian inscriptions which rose three to four hundred feet in the air.

After the Persian had been copied he went on to the second language, Elamite. The third language, Babylonian, was on the most dangerous and inaccessible part of the cliff face and could not be reached by courage alone. It required long strong ropes and ladders, both of which had to be brought into the area from outside. The attack on the third inscription was therefore postponed until he had worked out the Persian.

Here the dedication of a scholar sustained him as bit by bit he put together the pieces of the puzzle. When success came, in 1846, with the publication by the Royal Asiatic Society of his translation of the Persian inscription at Behistun, Rawlinson became famous. The sensation he created matched that of Champollion and his translation of the hieroglyphics. But Rawlinson was not alone in his achievements. Other scholars, notably Edward Hincks and the Frenchman Jules Oppert, had also gone a long way toward solving the mystery of the forgotten Persian script.

Even so, the most difficult part of the work was yet to come. When the ancient Persians had adopted the cuneiform symbols, they had used them as an alphabet, each symbol standing for a letter. But the oldest of the three scripts, the Babylonian, was not alphabetic at all. As with hieroglyphics, a sign might stand for a syllable or word—and not always for the same syllable or word. This habit of changing signals apparently at will in the middle of an inscription proved so confusing that the work of translation came to a near standstill.

Help was to come from a totally unexpected quarter, but to show how it happened we must make a slight detour from the inscriptions themselves. While the translators were mulling over their symbols, their colleagues were going on with the equally laborious work of digging. In 1842, Paul Emile Botta, another archaeologist who had accepted a diplomatic appointment to help him work in a foreign country, started excavating at Kuyunjik, in Mesopotamia. As French consular agent to the nearby city of Mosul he had few official duties and could spend an entire year at Kuyunjik. This was time enough to dash most of his hopes. In a year's digging he found almost nothing.

Botta's generosity in paying other men to dig soon aroused curiosity, and an Arab from a nearby village stopped to ask what the Frenchman wanted. Inscribed bricks? Nothing easier. He would like to recommend to Monsieur Botta the nearby village of Khorsabad, where such bricks were obtainable by the thousand with a few turns of the spade.

Rather half-heartedly, Botta sent several men to Khorsabad to try their luck. He expected little, and another failure would not have disappointed him. Instead of failure, however, his men had a stunning success. The discoveries he had been seeking for the past year could be made at Khorsabad with incredible ease. Within a week his men had uncovered the walls of an Assyrian palace which had belonged to the ancient King Sargon. Sculptures, weapons, interesting objects of every kind turned up. For the first time a modern scholar had a chance to see from the sculptures what those dreaded scourges of the ancient world, the Assyrians, looked like.

In France the excitement matched Botta's own. It was fortunate that it did, for the young consul needed all the support his countrymen could provide. The Pasha of Mosul, judging Botta by his own standards, could conceive of only one reason for digging—gold. From time to time he ordered the work stopped, imprisoned the diggers, and despite Botta's diplomatic status, created the most undiplomatic difficulties. The sculptures already dug up began to crumble for lack of care. Only Botta's own tireless energy, along with the help and encouragement given by his fellow Frenchmen, enabled him to fight off the Pasha and finally to ship a heavy cargo of sculptures and bas-reliefs to Le Havre.

Among the excavators who followed Botta, Austen Henry Layard was one of the most strikingly successful. Layard too had the prime requisites for a successful archaeologist in the Mesopotamia of the middle nineteenth century—youth, energy, intelligence, and courage. As a consequence of these qualities he acquired possibly the most important gift of all, luck. He had little money, and he had to fight against the same hardships Botta had encountered, as well as against a corrupt politician of the same kind. But that luck of his spared him the miserable year of failure which Botta had suffered.

He began to dig at Nimrud, and in a single day discovered two Assyrian palaces like those Botta had dug up at Khorsabad. Excavation of the palaces revealed great winged statues of lions and bulls like those Botta had found. Portable works of art were exactly what Layard wanted, and massive though these

An Assyrian statue in
a museum

stone creatures were, they were definitely portable. They were shipped to England, which now had its Assyrian monuments to match those of the French.

Layard did not stop here. From his excavations at Nimrud he learned that the Assyrians constructed their buildings on a platform of sun-dried brick. He therefore boldly tackled Kuyunjik, where Botta had failed so dismally. First he dug down to the brick platform, then cut trenches horizontally in different directions until one of them hit a wall. Following this he eventually reached what turned out to be the palace of Sennacherib, in the Assyrian fortress of Nineveh. Poor Botta, on the verge of success without knowing it, had been digging all around the palace. Inside, Layard uncovered the greatest treasure of all—thousands of clay tablets, part of the library of the Assyrian King Ashurbanipal.

We can imagine Botta tearing out his hair at the news and cursing the Englishman's luck. But it is clear that if Layard had lacked the boldness and the intelligence to tackle the mounds in the particular manner he did, luck would have frowned instead of smiling upon him.

In 1853, another quality needed for successful archaeological research was demonstrated by Hormuzd Rassam, Rawlinson's assistant. Rassam, who dug in the same area, had not only some of Layard's energy and luck, but also the determination once associated with Captain Kidd and the buccaneers who ravaged the Spanish Main. When he realized that a French rival, Victor Place, was approaching the very spot where he himself wanted to dig, he rushed in, tore up the soil, and had a stroke of fortune so outrageous that it seemed absolutely unfair. He too uncovered a palace, a great structure that had once belonged to Ashurbanipal himself, and in it, undisturbed for three thousand years, lay the remainder of the Assyrian monarch's great clay library.

Most of the tablets were copied from the older tablets of the Babylonians. A great number were about religion, some dealt with magic, which in ancient times was equivalent to what might be called Applied Religion, and a small number were about mathematics, astronomy, and medicine. The contents, naturally, were known to neither Layard nor Rassam, for we must recall that the written language of the Babylonians was at that time still a mystery. It did not remain a mystery long once the tablets of the library were examined and classified. Many turned out to be dictionaries. They were undoubtedly intended for the use of Assyrian scribes, and they were extremely useful in enabling Rawlinson and other scholars to solve the puzzle of the Babylonian symbols.

This puzzle, we may note, seemed to many people so definitely unsolvable that they devised a test which is common enough in other branches of science but struck archaeologists of that time as unique, and possibly unfit for a group of gentlemen to apply. In chemistry, for example, if you wish to test the reliability of an analytical method, you send a sample for analysis to several different laboratories and see if they all report the same result. In the same spirit of scientific doubt, the Royal Asiatic Society sent a sample of Babylonian cuneiform to Rawlinson, Hincks, Oppert, and Fox Talbot, another scholar. Working independently, all four men produced practically the same translation, which was published in 1857. After this there could be no further question as to whether the long-dead Babylonian language had been correctly translated.

Mystery, however, was not entirely done away with. Why did the Babylonians and Assyrians need dictionaries in the first place? Why could a single sign have several different meanings? Why, for that matter, can a single English word represent several quite different meanings, or why may a single idea be represented by different words?

In general, the answer to all these questions is the same. Neither modern English nor ancient Babylonian cuneiform were wholly invented by the people who used them. Both were largely borrowed from previous languages. English words have been derived from Anglo-Saxon, Latin, Norman French, various strains of German, and a number of other languages as well. In the world of 2000 B.C., written languages were scarce, and it appeared to Edward Hincks, who had taken an active part in untangling the problems of the Persian and Babylonian languages, that the Babylonians had borrowed their symbols from a much older people. In 1869 the French scholar Jules Oppert, recalling the existence of ancient inscriptions in which Mesopotamian monarchs styled themselves "King of Sumer and Akkad," asserted that these people were the Sumerians.

Between this bold guess and its confirmation only a few years elapsed. In 1877 another French consular agent, Ernest de Sarzec, began excavations at the mounds of Telloh, and uncovered the ancient Sumerian city of Lagash, along with many stone statues of its king, Gudea, and two baked clay cylinders inscribed with a form of cuneiform which had preceded the Babylonian. Now the civilized world had a chance to be astonished at the art and literature of a powerful kingdom so ancient that its existence had apparently been unknown even to the Greeks and Romans.

For the next twenty-three years De Sarzec continued his explorations, uncovering more and more material about the Sumerians. Meanwhile, during the last three decades of the nineteenth century other sensational discoveries were taking place so rapidly that blank areas in the picture of the ancient world seemed to be filled in almost every day. Discoveries were made by men of all kinds—retired generals, wealthy business men, self-trained amateurs, as well as professional archaeologists. In London, for example, a man with the commonplace name of George Smith became a self-taught expert on Babylon. Working in the Assyrian Department of the British Museum, Smith came across a clay tablet which told the story of Gilgamesh, first a Sumerian and later a Babylonian hero, who sought his ancestor Utnapishtim to find the secret of eternal life. Smith found on this tablet a reference to a ship resting on a mountain, and read about the sending forth of a dove. The similarity to the Biblical story of Noah was striking, and created a sensation when he revealed it.

But the story on the tablet was incomplete, and Smith deduced that it was a part of a larger narrative, which he might reasonably expect to find in the library of Ashurbanipal. A London newspaper raised funds to send him to Mesopotamia, and there, in 1873, in only a few days, in the library of clay tablets at Kuyunjik he found most of the missing parts of the epic of Gilgamesh.

A startling epic it was. Utnapishtim, it turned out, had not only lived through a great flood, but had undergone a number of other experiences very much like those to which Noah was subjected. There were in fact so many points of similarity between the story of Utnapishtim and the Biblical account of the Flood that there could be no doubt of Noah's literary origin. He was Utnapishtim in a different guise. To a world which had for centuries believed in the Bible as a unique document of divine inspiration, the discovery that one of its most fascinating narratives had been part of the general mythological heritage of early Mesopotamia came as a shock.

Other excavators were not idle. In the early eighties, Hormuzd Rassam dug up the records of that King Nabonidus already mentioned as the first archaeologist. Nabonidus had excavated the temple of Shamash, the Sun God, built by King Ur Nammu fifteen centuries before his own day. With each discovery about these remarkable early civilizations, interest in the Babylonians and Sumerians increased. And with the finding at Tell el Amarna, in Egypt, of clay tablets containing the fourteenth century B.C. diplomatic correspondence between Egypt and Babylon, a mass of detailed information became available.

One of the most surprising finds occurred at Bogazkoy, in the northeastern part of Asia Minor. Bogazkoy had been discovered by Texier, a Frenchman, in 1834, and studied more or less sporadically in the decades that followed. In 1894 another French archaeologist announced the discovery of tablets covered with cuneiform writing of a new kind. In 1906 a German expedition under the supervision of H. Winckler began thor-

A Hittite hieroglyphic inscription on stone

[105]

ough excavations and revealed that Bogazkoy had been the capital of an empire whose existence only Winckler and a few others had suspected—that of the Hittites. Thousands of clay tablets were found, dating from 1500-1200 B.C.

Translation of the Hittite cuneiform writing was accomplished by the Czech scholar Friedrich Hrozny in 1909. The tablets were documents outlining the Hittite law codes and concerning foreign affairs, the Hittite equivalent of the tablets at Tell el Amarna, and they shed considerable light not only on Hittite customs but on the relations of these almost forgotten people with their neighbors. Diplomats are by profession well trained in the art of adding irrelevant details to obscure what they are saying. As historians they can therefore be rather annoying. But if your chief interest is in the supposedly irrelevant details, you can be thankful that they talk so much, and that the Egyptian, Babylonian, and Hittite diplomats wrote so much.

During the same period, extensive excavations were undertaken by a German group under Robert Koldeway at Babylon. Koldeway brilliantly applied some of the most careful scientific methods known in his time to the complete excavation of the great walls and palaces of the city described by Herodotus, and confirmed much of the ancient Greek historian's report. Meanwhile, another German expedition under Dr. Walter Andrae was laying bare the remains of the Assyrian city of Asshur, as well as the even older temple ruins that lay beneath it. Together the two expeditions uncovered a fascinating wealth of information about life in ancient Mesopotamia.

World War I put a temporary end to digging. But in 1922 a joint British and American expedition under Sir Leonard Woolley began to dig at Ur of the Chaldees, shifting occasionally to another site, but returning to Ur frequently in the next decade. At Ur, Woolley discovered tombs which dated back long before the time of Abraham. These tombs, rich in gold and semi-precious stones, added further detail to what was known about early Mesopotamian cultures. And at Al' Ubaid, four miles away, Woolley excavated a Sumerian temple built by A-anni-padda, King of Ur, "son of Mes-anni-padda"—kings who had formerly been regarded as semi-mythical figures.

Other large expeditions were also active. As their work continued, it became clear that the First Dynasty at Ur, dated about 2800 B.C., did not represent the beginnings of civilization. Evidence accumulated about an advanced people who had entered the area a thousand years before the Sumerians. The names of Sumerian cities appear to have been derived from these previous inhabitants. And beyond the immediate forerunners of the Sumerians, artifacts have been found dating back to the Neolithic and even the Paleolithic Eras.

From all this archaeological labor, modern scholars have been able to picture the beginnings of culture in Mesopotamia and Asia Minor in a way that neither the Bible nor the Greek historians could. The early inhabitants had possibly entered the Bronze Age by 2600 B.C. or so, the time when the Sumerians left their mountain homes (exactly where they came from is still a mystery) to arrive on the scene.

The Sumerians took over and developed a flourishing civilization which lasted for possibly fifteen centuries. They invented cuneiform writing, and in many ways matched or surpassed the Egyptians. True, their paintings and sculpture were not of the highest artistic quality, although they did show great skill in carving, and this may give an erroneous impression to those who judge a people by what it has bequeathed to Western museums. But they could boast of other achievements of a high order.

They made use of, and further developed, such important implements as the plow and such means of transport as the sailing boat; they adapted the wheel for use in carts, developed to a surprising degree the key sciences of mathematics and astronomy, and devised and bequeathed to the Babylonians, and eventually to us, the sexagesimal system on which our reckoning of minutes and seconds is based. They knew the geometrical theorem about the square on the hypotenuse of a right triangle being equal to the sum of the squares on the sides—a theorem still credited to Pythagoras in our textbooks. They were skilled workers of copper and bronze, and weavers and dyers of cloth. They had, like the Egyptians, developed the practical chemistry of paints, perfumes, and cosmetics. They used enough drugs to fill a pharmacy.

They lived in perhaps a dozen large cities, each surrounded by a network of agricultural villages. As with all ancient civilized peoples, agriculture was the basis of their economic life, and they built an intricate irrigation system to ensure good crops.

They enjoyed music. One of the most famous archaeological finds is the elaborately decorated harp of Queen Shubad, the wood almost completely decayed in the course of forty centuries. From impressions left in the ground, modern science has been able to reconstruct it, and a handsome instrument it was. Clay tablets tell of drums and tambourines and wind instruments which were played both for enjoyment and for religious ceremonies.

Religion played a large role in Sumerian life. The Sumerians had accumulated an elaborate system of myths about the adventures and struggles of the gods, particularly of Enlil, god of the air. Their cities were built around great temples, each constructed atop a ziggurat or tower with terraces winding around it. The tower of Babel was the most famous of these ziggurats, although it was not intended, as the Biblical story has it, to storm the heavens. The ziggurats were artificial mountains, presumably symbolic of the original mountain homes of the Sumerians. Mountains played a large part in their religious life, as in the life of later peoples in the same area. (Recall the Biblical importance of Mount Sinai.)

Religion permeated Sumerian existence without completely overshadowing it. The Sumerians built their temples not as monstrous mausoleums for dead kings and queens, as the Egyptians did, but as actual places of worship. And because the chief priests were regarded as agents of the gods and were responsible for keeping track of the gods' property, the Sumerians developed cuneiform writing with which to keep accounts. From pictures of birds or fish or other animals which the gods owned, along with a number of marks to indicate quantity, the priests gradually developed a system of signs to denote words or syllables. The Egyptians may have borrowed the idea, although not the actual symbols, for their hieroglyphics. Later, the Babylonians took over the symbols.

Except for the names of kings and cities, the history of Sumer follows the already familiar pattern. The kings who ruled different cities fought continually, first one and then another becoming King of Kings. The cities of Erech, Kish, and Ur—the Biblical Ur of the Chaldees—were prominent in these endless wars.

About 1800 B.C. the Babylonians under Hammurabi brought Sumerian power to an end. Instead of destroying Sumerian culture, however, the Babylonians took it over, adopting not only the cuneiform symbols but much of Sumerian religion, such customs as the building of ziggurats, and all the skills which the Sumerians had achieved in the crafts of daily life as well as in mathematics and astronomy. The Babylonian way of life was in many respects a continuation of the Sumerian.

At about the time the Babylonian Empire was founded by Hammurabi, give or take a couple of centuries, the Hittites established their own empire in Asia Minor. The power of the Hittites was weakened by war—civil war, war with Egypt, war with the powers of Mesopotamia. About 1190 B.C. the Hittite kingdom was destroyed by invaders from the West, and more than three centuries later, the Assyrians overthrew the Babylonians.

Other ancient peoples such as the Phrygians, Scythians, and Cimmerians played a role in the military and political history of the period. As allies or mercenaries they took part in the killing and dying, and especially in the plundering for which many wars were then fought. But the words of the Biblical prophet were never truer: "They that live by the sword shall perish by the sword," and the Assyrians certainly lived by the sword. They were themselves overthrown by the Medes, the Medes in turn by the Persians, and the Persians by the Macedonians under Alexander the Great.

By the time of Alexander the very existence of the Sumerians, not to speak of their predecessors, was forgotten. But their cultural contributions remained. Their invention of cuneiform writing had suggested other forms of writing, and some of these had at last evolved into alphabets. Their achievements in arithmetic and geometry, their tables of heavenly motions, their skills in agriculture, metal-working, and many other crafts were passed on by way of the Babylonians to the Greeks and eventually to us.

We are accustomed, when we think of our heritage of the past, to marvel at the "miracle" of ancient Greece. But as a later miracle worker, Sir Isaac Newton, once said about himself, if he saw further than others it was because he stood on the shoulders of giants. The Greeks too stood on the shoulders of giants—such giants as the Sumerians and the Egyptians. In the past too many scholars have been ignorant of this fact or have conveniently forgotten it. When we see what the Greeks owed to others we can judge the pattern of ancient life more fairly. The intellectual heights the great men of Greece attained are not diminished thereby. But the apparent miracle of a small group of individuals standing so high while supported by nothing but thin air is at least partially explained.

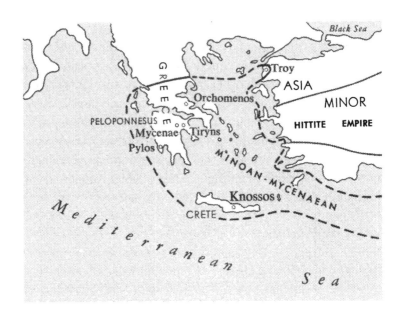

IX - THE AGE OF HEROES

WHAT THE BIBLE WAS TO RELIGION, THE ILIAD OF HOMER WAS TO
classical scholarship. Its poetry, revered for more than twenty-
five hundred years, had become the fountainhead and inspiration for all subsequent poetry. Its myths had been starting
points for Greek and Latin tragedy as well as for French and
English plays of the seventeenth and eighteenth centuries.
Scholars had studied each line, word, and syllable, and had debated endlessly the nature of its grammar and poetic imagery.
Seven Greek cities claimed to be Homer's birthplace, although
later scholarship doubted the claims of all seven on the ground
that Homer was possibly not a single person but a number of
poets. To express a low opinion of the *Iliad* was to be guilty

of blasphemy, and worse still of idiocy as a critic or poet. No
one dared do such a thing, except a few ignorant students bored
by the Greek grammar inflicted upon them in classical courses
of study.

And yet, with all this idolatry, few of the scholars who
studied his work thought of paying Homer the supreme com-
pliment. Homer was after all a poet, and poets were, almost
by definition, liars. The further from the truth they strayed
the higher their inspiration soared. Homer's tales of gods and
goddesses, of demigods and invulnerable heroes, were, in the
opinion of many, obvious inventions. His descriptions of chase
and combat were high art, but the essence of art is imagination. Not many would have thought of taking his words seriously as a description of events that really occurred.

Heinrich Schliemann did, for one. Born in 1822, he was,
from the age of seven, fascinated by the *Iliad* and determined
that some day he would discover the scene where its tragedies
had been acted out. He believed that not only had Troy existed
but all the heroes as well—Menelaus and Odysseus, Hector
and Achilles, and all the rest of them. And some day he would
prove his belief.

That day was delayed for forty years. Archaeological excavation of the kind he intended required money, and Schliemann's father was poor and addicted to drink. First Schliemann had to earn a living, then make himself rich. With an
excellent talent for business he succeeded beautifully in both
objectives, and while doing so traveled widely through North
and South America, Africa, and Europe, and also learned
more than a dozen languages in preparation for attaining his
archaeological goal.

His ability to pick up languages is of some interest. True,
he had a good ear and a good memory, for once he had hit

his stride he learned to speak and write Dutch, Spanish, and Portuguese fluently in six weeks of work on each. But to natural ability was added a high degree of will power and concentration. In order to remember words and grammatical expressions he practised reciting them so loudly that his neighbors complained and had him evicted. He even hired a man to listen to him, not caring in the least that nothing he said could be understood. The important thing was that his hired listener had the appearance of being attentive, and therefore stimulated him to do his best.

By 1870 he was prepared to dig. The year before he had married a young Greek girl who soon shared his archaeological interests and helped him devotedly in his work. The great question, however, was where to begin.

Homer's Troy had been covered with the debris of centuries, and the exact burial ground of the ancient city was a matter of dispute. Most scholars believed that the site was at a village called Bunarbashi, in Anatolia. Guided by his beloved Homer's description, however, Schliemann rejected the opinion of the experts, made an on-the-spot study, and decided that the best place to dig was at Hissarlik some miles away. There he hired a number of workmen and started to tear up the soil.

He had, in a way, too much success, for he found not one Troy, but seven. And all seven were at first disappointing. The earlier cities had been destroyed and later ones built upon the ruins—but which of these was Homer's Troy? Schliemann had no way of knowing, for at this time the methods of dating by pottery and other objects had not been worked out, and he was not sufficiently trained in archaeological and geological techniques to evaluate the evidence of the different layers. But in his day, of course, very few people were. Most of the "experts," even after his discoveries, continued to believe that he

Troy: remains of a tower and eastern section of fortification wall, built in Troy VI and still in use at the time of the Trojan War

was digging in the wrong place. No wonder that Schliemann was in no hurry to take their advice on any subject.

Continued excavation would later reveal not merely seven cities, but nine. Meanwhile, which of the seven was Homer's Troy? Unable to decide, he continued digging, examining the remains carefully. In the second and third levels from the bottom he found what had once been great walls and a great gate which showed signs of having been burned. The story of the burning of Troy leaped into his mind. This was the Homeric city he was looking for!

He was elated and yet disappointed. His finds were of great archaeological interest. But where was the golden treasure of Priam, King of Troy? He had seen no trace of it. Perhaps it had been stolen centuries ago, as the treasures of Etruscan and Egyptian kings had been stolen. It was useless to keep up the search for it too long.

The day before he had decided to give up work and admit defeat he saw in a layer of dirt a glint as of gold. Excitement leaped up within him, but he gave no sign. Speaking quietly to his wife, he had her dismiss the workmen with pay under the pretext that it was his birthday. And then he and his wife proceeded to uncover a dazzling treasure of golden diadems, bracelets, and goblets, numerous golden earrings, and thousands of small rings, as well as other articles of silver, copper, bronze, and electrum (a gold-silver alloy). Here at last, he was sure, was the treasure of which Homer had sung.

Again the civilized world was astounded by a great archaeological discovery. But, although Schliemann had revealed not a new world but a brave old one, like Columbus, he had not found the world he was looking for. He had trusted a bit too much to the guidance of Homer. The poet had spoken of a single Troy, the one Troy of which he had known, and Schliemann had tried to identify that city solely from Homer's account among those he had found.

Later work revealed that the oldest layer at Hissarlik dated back to between 3200 and 2600 B.C. Schliemann's "treasure of Priam" came from the second town, which had existed from 2600 or 2300 B.C. and had been destroyed by fire. The actual Troy of Homer's *Iliad* was in the first part of the seventh layer, which dated from 1300 or 1200 B.C.

Later and less excitable excavators could correct Schliemann's mistakes. It must be recalled, however, that he himself had no previous grand-scale excavations of multilayered cities to guide him. And in many respects he was in advance of his time. He preserved everything he found, kept unusually full records, made numerous drawings, and took photographs of all important finds. He also published full accounts of his expeditions as soon as he could get his results in proper shape.

Schliemann went back to Troy several times, his final excavations taking place in 1890, the year of his death. After his first expedition, he had trained archaeologists to assist him. Although none of his later discoveries at Troy matched in excitement those of his first expedition, his assistants proved their value in interpreting the finds. W. Dörpfeld, who was with him the year of his death, continued working at Troy until 1894.

For some time archaeologists were in sharp conflict over the meaning of Schliemann's discoveries. Some minimized their importance, regarding all the cities of Troy as much later than the one Homer had described. Actually, their significance was quite the opposite. At Troy Schliemann had discovered not only Homeric but pre-Homeric civilizations.

Schliemann possessed not only intelligent enthusiasm but an uncanny ability to scent good places to dig. For Troy was only his first success. In 1876, guided this time by Pausanius, another ancient Greek writer, he turned his attention to Mycenae, in Greece. Here he hoped to find the tomb of Agamemnon, leader of the Greeks in the Trojan War, and his faithless wife, Clytemnestra. He did in fact discover five graves, even richer in treasure than his finds at Troy. Once again he thought he had been guided aright. And again it was to turn out that he had found not the treasure he expected but a more ancient one, dating from before the days of Homeric heroes.

Later Schliemann dug at Orchomenos, another Greek city mentioned by Homer, and at Tiryns, not far from Mycenae. At both places he made exciting discoveries. At Orchomenos he excavated the treasury of Minyas, an ancient king. At Tiryns, renowned as the birthplace of Hercules, he discovered the foundations of a great palace and dug up pottery and wall paintings that resembled those he had excavated at Mycenae.

The Lion Gate (left) and
the Tomb of Clytemnestra
(below) at Mycenae

Other archaeologists were by this time intensely interested in Grecian sites. Some interesting finds had been made in Crete, a narrow island, more than a hundred and fifty miles long, off the southeast tip of Greece, and evidence was beginning to indicate that Crete had played a great role in pre-Homeric times. Schliemann made plans to dig there. But attempts to arrange with the owner of a hill for the right to excavate dragged on, and in 1890 Schliemann died, leaving the discoveries of Crete to his successors.

Jealous rivals were always ready to point out Schliemann's faults, real or fancied. He was stubborn, he was fanatical, he knew little about archaeological methods, he was in fact not much of an archaeologist at all. But his chief fault in their eyes was that he was so often right when they were wrong. His so-called "stubbornness" led him to trust his own mind instead of theirs, and resulted in his making sensational discoveries in areas which they considered archaeologically barren. His "fanaticism" drove him to keep on working against difficulties when more "reasonable" men might have given up. True, he lacked an extensive background in archaeological training. But he was honest enough to recognize his own weakness. After the first expedition at Hissarlik he remedied it by securing the best assistance he could, and from one expedition to the next he learned more and more.

His ability to select the places where great finds awaited seemed at times almost uncanny. His successes, and the passionate devotion to his work which produced them, inspired an entire generation, archaeologists and non-archaeologists alike, and still retain their power to excite the minds of men.

By the time Schliemann died, considerable interest had been aroused in the Mycenaean civilization. Had it originated in Greece, or was it a copy of some other ancient civilization?

What were its relations to the better-known civilizations of Egypt and Mesopotamia? Without excavations in Crete it seemed impossible to solve these problems.

In 1900, Arthur Evans began to work at Crete. At this time Evans was forty-nine years old, with a distinguished career already behind him. Having studied both at Oxford and at the University of Göttingen, in Germany, he had that complete academic training which Schliemann lacked, and had become one of the foremost archaeologists in Great Britain. Intrigued by the discovery of stones with what appeared to be primitive writing on them, and inspired by a belief that Crete was one of the centers of Greek civilization, he dug at Knossos, not far from the north shore of the island, almost halfway between its eastern and western ends.

Unlike Schliemann, Evans was lucky from the very beginning. In two months he uncovered the ruins of a great building which he identified as the palace of Minos, legendary king of Crete, famous as a lawgiver to whom even the greatest of the gods went for advice. But these ruins stretched over a number of acres, and a few weeks of digging would only begin to reveal their secrets. Year after year Evans continued to dig at Knossos, where he uncovered the remains of a long-lived Bronze Age civilization previously unknown. Below that civilization he found layers of soil, twenty feet thick in all, which contained artifacts created by men of the Neolithic Era. Eventually, the excavations he carried out revealed the history of Knossos from about 2900 to 1100 B.C. Evans's achievement at Knossos surpassed everything he had done in his previous career.

It was the sensational discoveries of the Bronze Age civilizations, however, that aroused public interest. For Crete had been the scene of mythical events familiar to the European

The palace at Knossos, Crete

civilized world from the time of Homer on. In Crete, King Minos of Greek mythology had built a great labyrinth to house the Minotaur, a monster with the body of a man and the head of a bull. Here the Athenians had been forced to send each year as a sacrifice seven young men and seven maidens, until Theseus had killed the monster, and, guided by a thread which the king's daughter, Ariadne, held at the other end, escaped from the hitherto deadly labyrinth.

Evans found a maze of buildings with so many differently shaped rooms and confusing corridors, on so many levels, that a stranger might easily have lost himself within them for weeks on end. He found paintings of the so-called "bull-dancers," which showed men and girls leaping over bulls in a dangerous game which might have been part of a religious ceremony. Mainland Greeks, who heard of the wonders of the palace, might easily have considered it a labyrinth designed to trap the unwary, and their primitive minds could without difficulty have transformed the dancers into sacrificial victims, the bull into a monster.

Evans found more. Uncovering great walls, impressive stone steps, and imposing columns, he showed that Crete had been at its peak the home of a rich and highly developed civilization, with unusually skilled craftsmen and artists. Three to four thousand years after its creation, Cretan art has an immediate appeal to modern men and women, to some people an appeal even beyond that of classic Greek art. After a time, however, there had been signs of deterioration. On their apparently impregnable island the rulers of Crete had accumulated perhaps too much wealth for their own good, had developed a love for luxurious living which made them unable to resist the invaders against whom they had long prepared their defenses. Eventually Crete was attacked, burned, and plundered.

Where had the civilization originated? Apparently not in Asia Minor, although this belief was once held. Nor in Egypt, despite the fact that Cretans and Egyptians both used the Mediterranean as a highway. We may recall that in 1889 Flinders Petrie found in Egypt Mycenaean and Aegean pottery mixed with Egyptian remains of the Eighteenth Dynasty. By this and later finds Petrie was able to establish relations among Egyptian, Cretan, and Mycenaean civilizations. But this did not prove that one of these civilizations had been derived from the others. There were too many differences between Cretans and Egyptians.

The great similarity between the objects found at Knossos and at Mycenae strongly indicated that the two cities had close ties. Was one a colony of the other? Did the rulers of

Crete, with their great sea power, conquer Mycenae and impose many features of their own culture, which Evans called Minoan, after Minos? At one time many archaeologists believed so. Now they have begun to doubt the theory of Cretan conquest. The Mycenaeans might have absorbed Minoan culture gradually, from commercial relations over a period of years. They might have paid Cretan artisans and craftsmen high wages to ply their skills on the Greek mainland. Or Mycenaean armies might have invaded Crete itself, long before the downfall of Knossos, and captured both objects of Cretan art and the men who made them.

The evidence so far is insufficient to decide such questions. But one great problem, which had helped lure Evans to Crete in the first place, and had baffled him to the end, has been solved since his death, thanks to the efforts of brilliant workers who followed him.

In 1937, Constantine Kourouniotis, of the Greek Archaeological Service, and Professor Carl W. Blegen, an American archaeologist, joined in an investigation of the Peloponnesus, the area in the south of Greece. Ancient royal tombs of the Mycenaean period had been found, and the two men hoped to locate the palace where the buried individuals had lived. After searching for two seasons, they chose a flat-topped hill, at Pylos, four miles from the sea. On the very first day of digging, they found the thick stone walls of a building, fragments of Mycenaean pottery, and most exciting of all, several clay tablets in a script previously found only on the island of Crete. Within a few days they had unearthed close to six hundred tablets, all in this same script, known as Linear B.

War interrupted both the excavations and the publication of their results, and it was not until 1951 that the tablets were published, and 1952, seven years after Dr. Kourouniotis had died, that Professor Blegen was able to return to the work. In six years he uncovered a palace which had apparently been destroyed by fire around 1200 B.C. In size and splendor it equalled the palaces of Mycenaea and Tiryns. In addition, it had a special interest all its own. For it appears, although this is not certain, to have been the home of that King Nestor of whom Homer wrote, the sage king who was a friend of Odysseus and gave advice highly prized by all the Greeks—despite the fact that Nestor's name has not been recovered.

But the tablets are in many respects more important than the palace. During his years of excavation on Crete, Evans, too, had dug up tablets, more than two thousand of them, covered with picture symbols. Because of a slight resemblance to Egyptian hieroglyphics these have also been called hieroglyphics, although they are nothing of the kind. The word, we may recall, means "priestly writings," and the Cretan scripts apparently were not religious at all, but served as records of inventories or commercial transactions. Known as Cretan Linear Script A and Linear Script B, they remained complete mysteries, related to each other, but apparently to no other form of writing.

Many scholars tried to solve the scripts on the assumption that they were in Etruscan, Egyptian, or Hittite. They failed. Some believed that the scripts might be in Greek, but Evans disagreed, and his word carried considerable weight. Meanwhile it had become clear that Linear A was an earlier form, used from about 1700 to 1500 B.C., and that the symbols of Linear B were derived from those of Linear A.

With the discovery of the scripts on the mainland, a significant fact was added. For these tablets of King Nestor's palace, which belonged to the Mycenaean culture, were all in Linear B. Investigation had shown that the Mycenaean culture was Greek. The implications of this fact were clear to Michael Ventris, a successful young British architect who had an interest in archaeology. "What," asked Ventris, "is historically more incongruous, a Knossos which writes Greek, or a Mycenae which writes 'Cretan'?" To Ventris the answer was plain. Linear B was almost certainly Greek. He proceeded to confirm his conclusion.

Like Champollion and other translators of unknown scripts before him, Ventris found it useful to learn many languages, choosing those that might be most closely related to the one he was trying to decipher. He found useful hints in the script of ancient Cyprus. The Cypriote script of 400 B.C. was a syllabary; that is, of its fifty-five symbols, five stood for vowels and the other fifty for syllables, which were combinations of consonants and vowels. Linear B was also a syllabary, and Ventris was able to apply to it much of what he learned from Cypriote.

The tablets at Pylos were inscribed with sketches which could be compared with the script. A man and woman might represent the Greek *pater* and *mater,* father and mother. A three-legged stand for a cooking pot suggested the Greek *tripodes.* By trial and error Ventris was able to find a whole series of familiar Greek words and proper names:

te-se-u or Theseus

ko-no-so or Knossos

a-ta-na or Athena

In some cases the similarities are less evident. The Greek of the Linear B dialect, or Achaean, was considerably different from that of Plato eight hundred years later, or even from that of Homer. But it *was* Greek. The riddle had been solved brilliantly.

It might have been solved even earlier if war had not delayed publication of the Linear B tablets of Pylos. In the

United States, a Brooklyn College linguist, Alice E. Kober, was on the trail of the answer. She showed the existence of masculine and feminine genders in Linear B and established the beginning of a phonetic pattern. But she died in 1950, a year before Professor Blegen published.

Ventris himself was killed in an automobile accident in 1956 at the age of thirty-four, a tragic loss to archaeology. Nevertheless, the work he had already accomplished was of tremendous value. He found in the Achaean tablets names of occupations which have given students a new picture of the Greek Bronze Age. The Mycenaeans and Cretans had words for armorers, bowmakers, goldsmiths, stokers, oarsmen, long-shoremen, tailors, doctors, supervisors, and property owners. From these and the other words he translated, the broad outlines of a civilization emerge.

The unexpected nature of these discoveries gives a new clue to some of the national relationships that may have existed in the years from 2000 B.C. on. So far, the only tablets found in both scripts, as had long been suspected, have contained only lists, inventories, and similar business records. Valuable as these are, no epics, no religious or mathematical texts have been discovered such as the Babylonians and Egyptians produced during the same period. Only further digging can tell whether such literary and scientific texts actually exist. So far, although more than two thousand tablets of Linear B have been found, those in Linear A number less than two hundred.

Crete and the Grecian mainland remain full of promise as sites for excavation, and the discoveries of Schliemann, Evans, and Blegen may yet be equalled or surpassed by the spades of archaeologists now unknown.

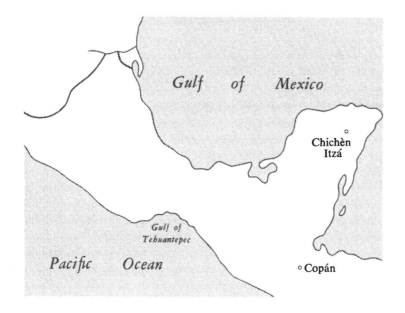

X-ARCHAEOLOGY
DISCOVERS AMERICA

WHEN COLUMBUS SAILED WEST IN 1492 TO DISCOVER A BRAVE NEW
World whose existence had been unknown to civilized Europe,
he linked it with the Old World in bonds which soon became
too strong to break. American gold poured into Europe and
stimulated kings and adventurers to frenzied activity. European
inventions, especially of weapons, trickled slowly across the
Atlantic to teach native Americans new ways of living and
dying.

The Spanish adventurers who followed Columbus discovered at least three distinct civilizations native to the Western

Hemisphere and then proceeded to destroy all three, while the more intellectual among them chronicled the symptoms of the death agony. Of these three civilizations, those of the Aztecs and the Incas were remembered for the golden booty they yielded. The achievements of the Mayas, on the other hand, were forgotten even by their descendants, who continued to live among the ruins of splendid old cities, while palaces and temples were overrun by the lush vegetation of tropical jungles.

It was apparent that civilizations do not spring from the ground as Minerva sprang from the head of Jove, vigorous and full grown. But the Incas had no written language in which history might be recorded, and the Aztecs apparently possessed one for only a few centuries. Moreover, the Aztecs were a relatively small group of Indian tribes. The written documents they left are incomplete, and give only a vague picture of what happened in Mexico.

There was another difficulty which applied to both Aztec written history and the accounts of Incan tradition. Both were composed for the benefit and convenience of priests and officials. They omit the details which most interest us. They tell which king overthrew his rivals and sacrificed ten thousand prisoners, but they mention only incidentally the manner of weaving or making pottery, or the conditions of life among the common people. As "authorized" stories of wars and revolutions they were slanted in favor of the government which authorized them. They also mingled fact and myth so completely that it sometimes becomes difficult to decide which is which. They are reliable only when their word receives independent confirmation.

Without objective historians there could be only one trustworthy record—the archaeological. But at the time of the

Spanish conquerors archaeology itself had not yet been born. No one knew how to interpret the numerous remains of the past which were so easily found.

Archaeology therefore had to become at least an infant science before the world could acquire a better knowledge of the Aztecs, the Incas, and the forgotten Mayas. A number of travelers in Central and South America stumbled across the ruins of great and impressive cities, were astonished at the marvels they saw, and then lost interest because there was no gold. Of archaeological treasures they had no conception.

By 1839, however, the archaeological discoveries in Pompeii and Egypt had become widely known. A young American lawyer, John L. Stephens, became interested in the growing new science and traveled through Egypt, Greece, and the Near East, to see the remains of ancient civilizations with his own eyes. Meanwhile, vague accounts of abandoned cities in Latin America did reach the United States and Europe. These accounts fired Stephens's imagination to the point where he was willing to brave the dangers of tropical jungles to see these fabled cities. Like many another student he secured a subsidy for the expenses of exploration from the United States Government. An appointment from President Martin Van Buren made him Special Confidential Agent to Central America with a mission to investigate the possibility of building a canal across Nicaragua, a possibility which was not realized until more than half a century later.

Stephens was fortunate in another way as well. No artist himself, he was acquainted with Frederick Catherwood, an English artist who had spent ten years in Europe sketching antiquities. Catherwood was a fine draughtsman and appeared to be just the person to make a pictorial record of the Mayas. Together the two men sailed south.

They landed in Guatemala in the middle of a three-way civil war which in most places was more like banditry than war. Reserving their spirit of adventure for more important affairs, they prudently tried to ride away on muleback from the fighting, only to be thrown into jail by a drunken officer. Released when the officer sobered up, they hurried on with Indian guides. After cutting their way through jungles, dragging themselves through muddy swamps, and climbing over mountain passes, they eventually reached the village of Copán, in Honduras, near which interesting ruins had been reported. From Copán they continued their slow and painful progress behind a guide who cut his way through the thicket of vines and underbrush with a machete, to find themselves at last in the middle of an ancient Mayan city overgrown with tropical vegetation.

Their first reactions were of delight and awe. Then came a feeling of despair. The ruins were so great, the inscriptions and designs on the monuments so weird and complicated, that it appeared hopeless to attempt a complete description. How could they set down in a few notebooks and sketchbooks a faithful record of what had obviously been a great and splendid civilization? They had in fact discovered more than they could digest mentally.

Nevertheless, they set to work and immediately found themselves in trouble. The city was on a tract of land which belonged to an old man who lived nearby, and he soon decided that he would not have any strangers drawing sketches on his property. To pacify the old gentleman, an important sedative was needed—money. Stephens supplied it, buying the entire city, ruined palaces and temples included, for fifty dollars. He was then able to study the ruins with no further interruption save that from the jungle itself.

The more he and Catherwood worked, however, the more disheartening became their task. The ruined buildings were so numerous and the sculptured columns and pillars were decorated in so complicated a fashion that to give even an incomplete picture was work for a dozen artists. In addition there were physical hardships. The jungle was hot, its roots and vines covered the inscriptions and twisted them out of place, and perhaps worst of all, the muggy air always swarmed with biting insects. Catherwood's artistic difficulties were multiplied by the need to draw in hundred-degree weather while wearing gloves.

As if all this were not enough, Catherwood also ran into a psychological obstacle. He was accustomed to the art of Greece and Rome and Egypt. He had never before encountered designs so foreign to his spirit and pencil. As art they at first made little sense, and how could he set down patterns without having some idea of their artistic meaning? How can a translator set down in English the meaning of a passage which he himself does not grasp, even though he knows all the words?

Catherwood's pencil was continually falling into its accustomed patterns of movement, obliterating some of the strangeness of these extremely strange designs, trying to impress his own sense of artistry on the one actually present, shaping the lines despite his will into something more familiar. It was a tendency he had to fight, and he helped conquer it eventually, after much hard work, with the aid of a *camera lucida,* a device which cast an image of light and shade on his paper to guide his pencil. Meanwhile, as Catherwood drew, Stephens explored, chopping his way from one monument and temple to another, and taking notes as rapidly as his own pencil could move. After Copán the two men visited other ruins, giving hasty descriptions of the wonders to be seen, and work-

ing at a steady pitch of excitement that made them forget
vicious mosquitoes and inedible food.

In 1841 Stephens published a book on his travels and discoveries, *Incidents of Travel in Central America, Chiapas and
Yucatan*. On the individuals who thought of Indians only as
"savages" condemned to bite the dust, his revelations made a
tremendous impact. The book, which has recently been re-
issued, tore aside the curtain of ignorance built by centuries of
contempt and revealed the achievements of a once great people.
It became a best seller in the United States and Europe.

The book's effect on archaeology, however, was slight.
There was no obvious connection between the ruins of Mayan
cities and the excavation sites of the Old World. Thomsen and
Nillson and Worsaae had begun to put order into the studies
of prehistoric man in Europe. But prehistoric man in the
Americas did not fit into their picture. In no possible way
could he be related to the Ages of Man as known to European
archaeologists.

The interest which Stephens had aroused was kept alive
by two great works by an American historian, William H.
Prescott. His *History of the Conquest of Mexico,* published in
1843, and *History of the Conquest of Peru,* published in 1847,
both based chiefly on Spanish sources, not only narrated in
vivid fashion the dramatic events of the conquest, but brought
alive to their readers some of the wonders of the ancient Aztec
and Incan civilizations. From then on, knowledge of the native
American cultures was destined to increase steadily.

But for a long time, as far as actual exploration and archaeological study went, Stephens and Catherwood remained almost lone trail-blazers. A French explorer, Desiré Charnay,
traveled through Central America for twenty-five years from
1857 on and wrote an account of the ruins he had seen. It was

not, however, until 1881 that more advanced archaeological methods came to Central America. Beginning in that year, an English archaeologist, Alfred Maudslay, once more cut through the jungle, and no longer relying upon the skill of an insect-bitten artist, took photographs and made excellent casts of numerous inscriptions. The extensive report he published gave archaeologists material to work on.

By this time also, a partial key to the Mayan hieroglyphics had been found. It had been resting for some centuries in the Royal Academy of History in Madrid, and had been rediscovered only a short time before Maudslay made his journeys to Central America. Called *An Account of Things in Yucatan,* it had been written by Diego de Landa, a Spaniard who had become Bishop of Yucatan. While doing his best to exterminate the religion and culture of the infidels, he obtained from these same infidels all the information he could. Later scholars who used his materials could make headway in interpreting Mayan hieroglyphics, number systems, and calendar dates. There remains some disagreement about dates, and occasionally there is fierce conflict about the meaning of hieroglyphics. But from the clues that Diego de Landa provided and the inscriptions at least partly translated with their help, as well as from archaeological evidence, some of the Mayan history has been deciphered.

In 1885 another diplomatic appointee followed the trail that Stephens and Catherwood had blazed, encountering a few new dangers in addition to those which had beset the earlier pair. As consul to Yucatan, E. H. Thompson traveled through the land from one Mayan antiquity to another, leaving his wife and child behind him while he gathered information from the Indians and from the ruins themselves. A visit to Chichén Itzá, greatest of Mayan cities, inspired him to follow Stephens's

Above: Tree growth over ruined edifice of the Temple of Jaguars at Chichén Itzá;
Below: the same temple after excavation and clearing of jungle growth. To the right
are a castle, pyramid, and temple.

example and buy the ruins he wanted to study. But by this time the price of deserted cities had gone up, and he was unable to strike so good a bargain. For the right to excavate, he had to impoverish himself and his family.

His greatest single achievement was his work on the Sacred Well of Sacrifice. Into its dark and gloomy depths, reported Diego de Landa, the Mayan priests hurled beautiful maidens and handsome young men as sacrifices. Rich offerings for the use of the gods were tossed in along with the victims. Diego de Landa's tale had generally been regarded as a myth, but Thompson, aware from the discoveries of Schliemann and others how much truth there sometimes is in old stories, decided that the well was worth exploring, even at the risk of his own life.

And risk there certainly was. Thompson returned to the United States and prepared for his work by taking lessons in deep-sea diving. In his day, however, diving equipment was heavy and clumsy, and depended for its air supply on the hand pumping of a group of men in a boat above. There were no tanks of oxygen or compressed air. Thompson had a flashlight capable of working under water, but in the muddy sludge which was so easily stirred up at the bottom of the Sacred Well this was useless and was soon laid aside. Most of his diving was done in darkness, aided only by his sense of touch.

Before making his first descent into the well, however, Thompson began work with a bucket dredge furnished with steel jaws that opened and shut. The well was a large one, one hundred and eighty-seven feet across at its widest point, and about eighty feet deep. Actual diving operations would be simplified if he could first locate the area where the victims had been hurled.

The dredge, like his diving equipment, was advanced for

the nineteenth century, even though inefficient by modern standards. At first it brought up only mud, dead leaves, water-soaked branches, and occasional animal bones. And then, one day Thompson found, amid the mud and debris, small yellowish lumps of resin, a form of incense burned during sacrificial rites. It proved to him that the well had been used as Diego de Landa reported, and that he was on the right track.

Soon he had even more convincing proof. Obsidian knives, jade bowls, ornaments of many kinds came up. As the final piece of evidence, he fished up portions of a human skeleton.

The area of sacrifice had been located. But dredging was beginning to bring up less and less. It was time for Thompson and his assistant, a professional diver, to put on their suits and go down into the well.

They found that the dredge had removed a good part of the mud and left a fairly clean layer of rock. In many places the two divers could feel the limestone bottom of the well and explore its crevices with their own hands. The well itself was full of danger. Loosened by the water, rocks would tumble down around them in the dark, threatening both the divers and their air hoses. Once Thompson forgot to open his air valves and began to float to the surface. As he rose rapidly, the pressure decreased, and tiny bubbles of air began to fizz from his blood. Realizing what was happening, he hastily opened the air valves, thus escaping death, but his eardrums were injured and his hearing permanently impaired.

The objects he brought up repaid him amply for his troubles. They included masses of jade figures, gold and copper disks, darts with stone points, even bits of ancient fabric. There were few objects of nearly pure gold, and considering the risks and labor involved, it was possible that in terms of monetary value Thompson had made a bad investment. But in their aid to an understanding of the ancient Mayas they were archaeological treasures, worth, as Thompson said, the labors of a lifetime.

In his disregard of personal danger Thompson followed what had by now become a tradition with archaeologists. The fact that he impaired his own health and probably frightened his wife half to death, was to him of little importance compared to the discoveries he made.

Fortunately for them, most later explorers of ancient American civilizations were not called upon for quite so extreme a degree of heroism as to go grubbing for skeletons in the mud at the bottom of a deep, dark well. But other kinds of danger lay waiting for them. In 1909, Hiram Bingham, a young American, began his search in the Andes for what had been known as Vilcapampa, a famous city of the Incas. This fabled fortress had become the retreat of those Incas who had escaped the Spanish invaders, and when the last Incas had died, the city had been lost.

It may seem odd for an entire city to disappear without being buried. But we must remember the circumstances of the invasion of Peru, and the nature of the country. Vilcapampa was not only a military fortress but a religious retreat as well, and the Incas revealed no secrets about it. Situated among high mountain peaks and attainable only after a long passage through dangerous ravines and jungles, it was sought in vain for more than three hundred years.

Bingham, who later became Governor of Connecticut and Senator from that State, was in 1909 only a young graduate with the degree of Ph.D. He set out, like previous seekers for the city, with only the vaguest idea of its location, and with no experience in archaeological work. As a guide to archaeological etiquette he took with him a book, *Hints to Travellers*, pub-

lished by the Royal Geographic Society. When he came across
his first interesting ruins, he had to consult the book in order
to learn the proper procedure. He was informed that it was a
good idea to make careful measurements and take many photographs, which he did.

His first season of search resulted in no great discoveries,
but was useful experience. He clambered over steep cliffs,
crossed long slender bridges over ravines and rapids, cut his
way through gloomy jungles, and in talks with officials and
Indian peasants picked up hints about the location of old ruins.
When he went back in 1911, the experience brought him relatively easy success. On a peak called Machu Picchu he discovered great ruins which fitted the ancient descriptions of
Vilcapampa. Careful study, this time with the help of specialists, convinced him that he had indeed found the lost city.

Built over many generations, Vilcapampa, or Machu Picchu,
as it is now known, lies in the most inaccessible section of the
Central Andes. The precipices which lead to it rise straight
up for a thousand feet, and the approaches are difficult even
for experienced mountain climbers. For half of each year the
rapids of the Urubamba River, which must be crossed before
the peaks are reached, are completely impassable. The other
half of the year they are merely extremely dangerous.

It was the very inaccessibility of the region that induced the
Incas to choose it for a sanctuary. Without iron tools they constructed a Temple of the Sun, along with great fortifications
of huge blocks of stone, and living quarters for the Incas and
the Virgins of the Sun. Atop Machu Picchu and a neighboring
peak they built signal towers on which watchmen stood to
warn of the approach of enemies. No wonder the Spaniards
could not extend their conquest to this formidable place.

Like the great discoveries which preceded it, the finding

of Machu Picchu had a sensational effect. It stimulated the sending of further expeditions and helped make a study of the Americas part of archaeology.

From a study of the various records, archaeologists have been able to piece together an account of the relations between different Indian tribes in Mexico and Central America. The Aztecs played a prominent role only in the late stage of American history preceding the Spanish conquests. Prominent in the earlier history of the region are other tribal groups of which we can name merely a few, such as the Toltecs, the Zapotecs, and the Mixtecs, all of whom rose to power and fell again at different times.

The relation of all these peoples to the civilization of South America, to the early cultures which preceded them, and to the cultures of the Eastern Hemisphere remains a mystery. Materials needed to provide a solution are scattered in many places. North and South America contain enough known finds to keep the present small number of archaeologists occupied for a hundred years. Sad to say, however, what the archaeologists cannot investigate is not being entirely neglected. From the days of the Conquest on, fortune-hunters have been attracted by the treasures of the Incas and Aztecs. Each year, despite the efforts of Mexican and Central American governments, valuable sites are plundered and hundreds of ancient objects sold to tourists and collectors. In Mexico alone, archaeological treasures valued at about a million dollars are taken out of the country each year.

Fortunately for archaeology, however, an old enemy has come to its partial rescue. The fine art of forging antiques now lures tourists away from genuine Aztec and Incan craftsmanship. It is easier to imitate an Aztec bracelet than to find one, and tourists are made happier by flashy imitations than they would be by dull-looking genuine relics. None the less, as in Egypt, Italy, Greece, and the Near East, many objects containing precious metal, or adorned with precious stones, fall into the hands of thieves. Under these circumstances, the archaeologist is fortunate to find another kind of treasure—the old ashes and bones, the fragments of pottery and stone, all the trash and refuse which do not appeal to thieves and yet tell much of the story of human life. It is from such clues as these that he hopes finally to decipher the riddle of American prehistory.

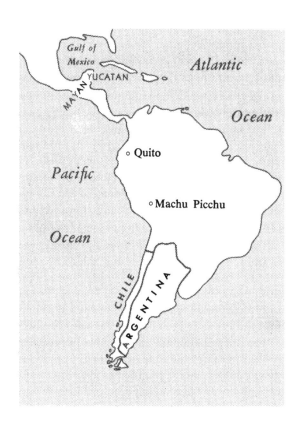

XI-THE NEW WORLD
IN ANCIENT TIMES

MEANWHILE, WHAT *has* THE ARCHAEOLOGIST LEARNED? WHAT does he know of the Incas and the Aztecs, and of their predecessors, beyond what the Spanish conquerors recorded?

Most scientists believe that man entered Alaska from Asia about twenty thousand years ago, crossing the narrow channel

[141]

now called Bering Strait. Very likely the first wave of immigrants was followed by others. Some immigrants may have crossed on the ice, others by boat. How many there were and for how long they continued to arrive we do not know. We do know that two or three thousand years ago the Eskimos who now inhabit the Arctic region came from Asia, making their way along the northern coast, and settling one island after another.

At any rate, until the first arrivals via Bering Strait, the Western Hemisphere appears to have been uninhabited by any human species. The only strangers to greet the newcomers were animals unaccustomed to hunters, and these must have been easy victims for men equipped with the weapons that had been developed by the close of the Old Stone Age.

There was, however, one enemy—the climate. At that time a large part of North America was covered by a sheet of ice, and possibly stimulated to move south by the cold welcome they received, some of the first settlers must have spread into Canada and down the west coast of North America. Eventually they poured over into Mexico and South America, as well as into the eastern part of the continent.

The evidence these early Americans left behind has been found at many sites throughout the Western Hemisphere. Stone and bone tools along with burned horse and sloth bones from a cave on the rim of an extinct volcano show that man reached the southernmost part of South America more than eight thousand years ago. But the journey down the length of the continent may have taken thousands of years. Charcoal of human origin from Tule Springs, Nevada, is thought to be more than 23,800 years old, and fossil deposits from Sandia Cave, in New Mexico, have been dated back 20,000 years. And in another cave, on an extinct volcano in Oregon, the remains have been found of seventy-five pairs of sandals made of sage-brush bark. Radiocarbon dating has here given an age of nine thousand years. If North American man was a savage in those days, at least he was not always a barefoot one.

From the evidence of animal bones it is clear that primitive man in North America, like his brother in Europe, was a good hunter. At first, possibly in the late stages of the Ice Age, or when the ice sheet was already retreating to the north, he hunted the elephant, the horse, and the camel, then native to the continent. His spears were tipped with characteristic points made of rough or chipped stone, unground and unpolished. Sometimes he used bone or ivory for his tools, but of these little trace has been found. Remains of these Paleo-Indians, "ancient Indians," as the most primitive men have been called, have been found in Mexico as well as in South America. But it is not at all certain that men at the same cultural stage in-habited different parts of the continent at the same time.

Slowly, as the Ice Age receded into the past, the great elephants died out, and bison took their place as man's most important animal food. At the same time, man began to depend less on hunting, as he learned to gather the fruit of wild plants. He learned also to grind and polish his stone tools, and he left behind numerous artifacts of bone, horn, and ivory. The first traces of this more advanced stage appear to date back to 9000 B.C. in Illinois and the Middle West. But the objects that have been dated are few, and the evidence is uncertain. Over most of the hemisphere advances appear to have taken place but slowly, and cultures remained primitive.

Some time in the second millennium B.C., agriculture in Middle America, the area which includes Mexico and Guate-mala, had advanced far enough to make life possible in per-manent villages. With food supplied mainly by domesticated plants, both hunting and food-gathering lost much of their previous importance. The art of making pottery was well advanced, and the stage of development corresponded to the New Stone Age, which had been reached earlier in Europe and Asia. A similar stage was reached in Peru at about the same time or a bit later.

Did advances in culture result from new waves of immigration from the Old World, or were they the contributions of the Paleo-Indians themselves? No general answer can yet be given, and the question is now under active investigation by a number of scholars. It is possible that the making of pottery and some of the improvements in making flints came from Asia. But many important advances were certainly made by the early Americans themselves. They learned to domesticate certain plants and a few animals which did not exist in the Old World.

Some early changes remained localized in narrow areas, others spread quickly over much of the hemisphere. About 10,000 years ago an early race of bison hunters lived near what is now Folsom, New Mexico, and the flint spearheads they used were of a type since found over thousands of square miles. The planting of maize spread all the way from Peru to the eastern part of the United States, and the making of pottery spread even further. When the bow and arrow were introduced, they soon became known over practically the entire hemisphere.

When England and Spain and other countries of Europe colonized the New World, most of the Indian tribes were at the New World equivalent of the Neolithic, or New Stone Age. But the Eskimos were only in the Mesolithic, or Middle Stone Age, while to the south, in Mexico, Central, and South America, the Western Hemisphere had advanced to the use of metal as a supplement to stone. In Peru the Indian tribes had domesticated Indian corn before 1200 B.C. They had by then organized a system of religion with animal and other gods reminiscent of the animal gods of Egypt. Later they erected great temples to these deities, including one to a Cat-God, and began to build stone edifices. They used bronze and learned how to cast gold, but the Bronze Age, as known in the Old World, did not appear.

These Indian tribes were the predecessors of the Incas, and much of the reputation the latter won was due to skills they acquired by inheritance. Egypt was a narrow strip of Nile valley plus desert; ancient Peru was mountain and jungle, plus desert. Split into small areas by natural barriers, it became the home of many peoples, who one after another grew strong and subjugated their neighbors, only to find that their success united enemies against them and led to their own overthrow. Not until the rise of the Incas, from about 1200 A.D. on, was a kind of unity imposed upon the entire territory. The Incas began their conquests in about 1440, less than a century before the arrival of their own conquerors. When the Spaniards appeared on the scene, the Incas still found it necessary to defend themselves from fierce Indian tribes on their borders.

Inheriting the achievements of all the cultures before them, the Incas tried to consolidate their empire. They built a wonderful system of highways, the longest of which was over four thousand miles from north to south, running the length of the Andes from Quito in Ecuador to Argentina and Chile, while east-west roads connected the Pacific Coast with the Eastern slopes of the Andes, where a second north-south highway ran for two thousand miles. These roads included suspension bridges that crossed canyons, and tunnels hundreds of feet in length that cut through mountains. Along them traveled the

Incan ruins of fortifications at Sacsahuaman, Peru. Notice the terraced structure.

fastest messengers the world had ever seen, running in relays that could cover in a day almost three hundred miles up and down steep mountains. Roads and messengers linked tens of thousands of square miles of country into one empire.

As remarkable as the roads was the irrigation system, which by means of great canals brought the water across many miles of mountain and desert. From the main canals the water was led into secondary channels and ditches and thence into the fields. Much of it was stored in reservoirs. The Incas understood the methods of irrigation and soil cultivation suited for their hilly fields and built terraces to prevent the soil from being washed away, even straightening roads and draining swamps where necessary.

In constructing their great cities the Incas brought blocks of stone weighing up to three hundred tons from quarries more than a mile away, moving them along without benefit of wheels, using only levers, ropes, possibly rollers, and above all, the patient strength of the workers. The great blocks themselves were shaped with such care that when they were fitted together, without cement, it was impossible to thrust the point of a knife between them.

The Incas had no writing, but they did have a peculiar mnemonic system of knotted cords which they used in recording the census, recalling historic events, or sending messages. Nowadays some of us tie strings around our fingers to remind us of things to do. The Incas had developed this simple device into a highly useful system. Their cords, called *quipus,* were made of alpaca or llama wool dyed in different colors. Each knot represented a number or an item to remember, and a trained messenger could easily translate a report of any kind into a pattern of knots at the beginning of his journey and retranslate the knots into words at journey's end.

Among the other inventions which the Incas treasured were a semi-decimal system of numbers based on five instead of ten, and a complicated and accurate calendar. As no useful calendar can be devised without a reasonably advanced knowledge of astronomy, it should come as no surprise that the Incas studied the motion of the sun and moon, as well as of prominent stars.

The people of their empire had learned to weave beautifully and to make wonderful pottery. These skills too the Incas had inherited, along with a knowledge of the plants and animals that could be raised in mountains and desert. In addition to using the wool of llamas, alpacas, and vicunas, they also grew and used cotton. Whether cotton developed first in the New World or the Old remains a mystery with which modern botanists have been much concerned, and equally mysterious is the manner in which it traveled half around the world, to be utilized in two different hemispheres for the making of fabrics. Less in need of explanation is the fact that the Indians of Peru, like the early peoples of the Old World, knew how to make a fermented drink and to use this in religious ceremonies.

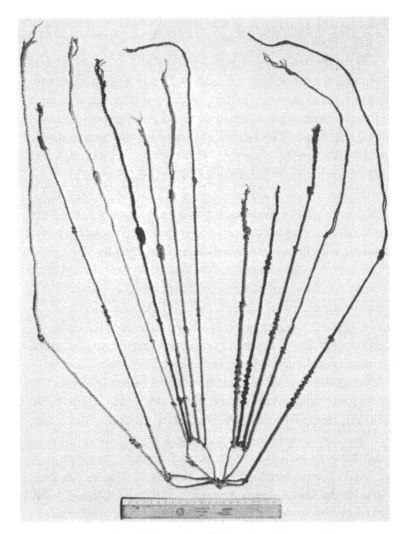

A Quipu, or Peruvian knot record

Among the Incas there was to a lesser extent that same division of labor we found among the ancient Egyptians. Most of the people were peasants. But there were specialists in different professions as well, from priests, warriors, physicians, surgeons, and astronomers, to civil administrators. The Incas were acquainted with many medicinal plants and relied greatly upon the coca leaf to deaden the sensations of pain, hunger, and fatigue. Their surgeons carried out such operations as trepanning of the skull to remove pieces of bone pressing on the brain, and limb amputations. Many of the patients recovered to talk about their operations in an age when antiseptics and antibiotics were unknown.

In different localities scattered through the mountains the Incas built fortress cities which they connected by the great roads. These great structures of stone were apparently intended to defend the empire from external enemies, mostly the still barbaric tribes who envied the more civilized Incas their wealth. The ability to plan such a defense testifies to the one great talent the Incas themselves had developed beyond what they took over from their predecessors. They had slowly developed a form of social and political organization more complex than those of many other Indian tribes, and they were able to impose this organization on the people they conquered.

They lacked not only writing, however, but a device which in the Old World was known at the beginning of the Bronze Age. Strangely enough they had never learned the advantages of that most obvious of inventions, the wheel.

While the civilizations of the Andes were developing, parallel civilizations were growing in Central America and in Mexico. In the area of modern Guatemala, Honduras, and Southern Mexico, the ancient Mayas, again taking advantage of skills developed by their forerunners, built a series of great religious centers, some of which may have been founded by the third century B.C. The era of great temple building, sometimes known as the Classic era, continued in the Valley of Mexico and the Guatemalan highlands to roughly 900 A.D. This era saw the climax of religious architecture, a high level of achievement in the arts, a general flowering of material culture, and the growth of city, as contrasted to village life.

Like most early cities in the Old World as well as the New, however, these did not resemble what we now call cities. They were built around temples, and depended for their existence on the farmers around them. Corn was the life of the Mayas. One old Spanish writer says that "they fell little short of making a god of it." The fact is that they *did* make a god of it, and an important god. In three months they grew enough to keep them and their families alive for a year. The rest of the time they could therefore labor for priests and chiefs, building the palaces, temples, and pyramids.

The Mayas had a peculiarly characteristic appearance which resulted from deliberate flattening of the forehead in infancy. This mark of beauty was often accentuated by cross-eyes, which some fond mothers tried to achieve by hanging little balls of resin between the eyes of their children. Apparently neither mark of beauty affected Mayan brains. For in addition to their art and their architecture, the Mayas had to their credit a pair of intellectual achievements that surpassed those of the Greeks and Romans, the Egyptians and Babylonians. They invented the most accurate calendar the world has ever seen, basing it on careful astronomical observations and brain-racking calculations. It has not been surpassed, even by our present Gregorian calendar which was adopted in 1582.

Their number system was on a level with their calendar. Devised several hundred years before Christ, it was based upon the number 20 instead of 10, and it outdid the number systems of the Greeks and Romans. The value of a numeral depended on its position, as in our own present system, and there was a symbol for zero. Western Europe had no such system until contact with Arabs in the Middle Ages.

Further north, the Indians of Mexico developed their own civilization, much of which came under the sway of the Aztecs. For them, as for the Mayas, corn was the giver of life, and among them, too, fertile land was scarce. The environment in which they lived was different from that occupied by the Mayas. They found a permanent solution to the problem of extending their agricultural land by the creation of artificial islands, called *chinampas,* in the lakes of the Valley of Mexico. The chinampas were held together by roots of reeds and trees, and the topsoil was renewed before planting time with mud from the shores or lake bottom. The chinampa system was so successful that it continues to exist to the present day.

Like the Incas and Mayas, the Aztecs and their predecessors were highly skilled architects, sculptors, and painters. They built pyramids and temples as well as islands. Their paintings, once undervalued as "primitive," later had a profound influence on the work of great modern Mexican artists, as well as on artists and sculptors in the United States.

Their craftsmanship showed great skill. With no source of tin, they alloyed copper with gold, to the misfortune of modern archaeologists, for the substance was later melted down by the Spaniards, to get the gold. They were fine potters —although they did not use the potter's wheel—as well as expert jewelers, weavers, and featherworkers.

The Aztec tribe was basically democratic. Families belonged to clans and the clans to the tribe. Clans managed their own affairs and at the same time had a voice in larger councils which discussed relations between allied tribes or with neighboring peoples outside. In the clans themselves the chieftaincy was obtained by popular election.

Democracy was not complete, for there were slaves—sometimes prisoners of war, more often criminals or impoverished people who had given up their freedom for food. A slave had his freedoms too, including the right to own property and other slaves. And slavery was not hereditary. The children of a slave were born free. Nonetheless, by the time of the Spanish conquest, much of the power was in the hands of the military and religious leaders, and democracy was on the wane.

The Aztecs grew cotton, smoked tobacco in a primitive form of cigarette, and obtained rubber from the guayule plant. They used the guayule rubber both as a glue and as raw material for rubber balls.

Like the Mayas they had a written picture language and paper on which to inscribe it. Their calendar had considerable religious significance, and both calendar and religion were as complicated as some systems of theology of the Middle Ages.

Their religion was, unfortunately, one of the darker aspects of Aztec life. By its great emphasis on cruel and bloody human sacrifice it cast a shadow on their history and art, and even today we find it difficult to forget how many tens of thousands of human victims were slaughtered to placate horrible gods. But outside of religion and warfare the Aztecs, like the Incas and the Mayas, were kind and accomplished, no more bloodthirsty than the ancient peoples of Africa, Europe, or Asia, no crueler than their Spanish conquerors or an eighteenth-century English mob licking its lips at a hanging.

The Indian civilizations have contributed much to the modern world, and it would be unjust to forget it. To learn the full story, archaeological excavations are continuing all over the New World, from Alaska through Canada, the United States, Mexico, and Central America, into wide areas of South America. Slowly the evidence is accumulating that will help answer the question of how the native American civilizations originated.

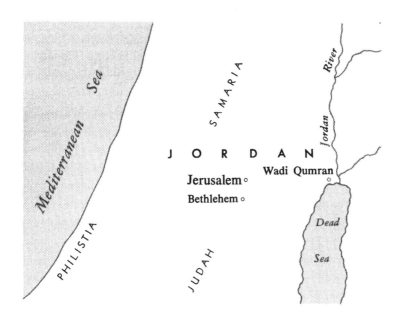

XII - THE DEAD SEA AREA
COMES TO LIFE

In the summer of 1947 the historic land of Palestine was lashed by severe political storms. All the contradictory interests which centered in that small country had flared up, the British Crown fighting a desperate but losing battle to maintain its power, while other groups fought to take over in its place. To a pair of young Arab goatherds grazing their small flocks in a valley known as the Wadi Qumran, near the Dead Sea, however, politics meant nothing in comparison with their personal affairs. Stories differ as to whether these personal affairs consisted of looking for a lost goat or pretending to do so as a cover for activities in smuggling. But whatever they sought, they found something they did not expect.

The Wadi Qumran is a miserable region, wild and desolate, with scrubby vegetation apparently unfit even for a goat to eat. Rocky cliffs rise on all sides, hollowed out by hundreds of caves which serve only as lairs for wild animals. It was into the opening of one of these caves that the goatherds strayed.

The inside of the cave was dark and foreboding. One of the boys threw a stone and prepared to run. They heard the sound of something being hit and then breaking. Beyond that, silence. No goat, no other living thing appeared to inhabit the cave.

They resumed their search elsewhere. The record is vague as to whether they recovered the missing goat. The next day, however, they did return to the cave, made sure it was still deserted, and crawled in, to find themselves between two unpleasantly close walls. On the floor stood eight large jars, some with covers on them. Thoughts of Ali Baba and the forty thieves must have crossed their minds.

Hoping for Ali Baba's good fortune, they looked into the jars. All were empty save one, and that contained only a large scroll and two smaller ones. With these they left in a hurry.

When they unrolled the large scroll it reached from one end of their tent to the other. Their friends and relatives were properly surprised, but not greatly impressed. After all, paper and parchment were not gold. They made other visits to the cave, discovered other scrolls to a total of seven, and then decided that although their treasure did not compare with that of Ali Baba, it might still have some value.

A dealer in Bethlehem examined the finds and sent them to the Monastery of St. Mark in Jerusalem, where they came to the attention of the Syrian Orthodox Metropolitan Samuel.

Vases from the caves where the Dead Sea Scrolls were found

Although not an archaeologist, the Metropolitan recognized their possible value and bought four of them, hoping to resell them later and devote the profits to improving the monastery.

Goatherds, dealer, and theologians did the usual haggling about price, but the goatherds threw in as a bonus a scrap of information which was more valuable than the scrolls themselves: they described the location of the cave to the people in the monastery.

Meanwhile, the other three scrolls were offered to Professor E. L. Sukenik of the Hebrew University of Jerusalem. Professor Sukenik was at once interested merely on hearing their description, but between him and the scrolls were a number of barriers: a cordon of British soldiers, half a dozen fighting groups, each with its own brand of martial law, and bands of marauders who took advantage of the general disturbance to kill and loot. In addition, Professor Sukenik lacked money. A large sum was finally raised with the aid of fellow scholars who had wealthy and influential friends. Getting past soldiers, murderers, and thieves to reach the dealer, complete the purchase, and return with the scrolls seemed impossible, but this feat too Professor Sukenik accomplished in dramatic fashion.

In April 1948, after he had taken time to examine the scrolls and was convinced of their authenticity and value, he announced their discovery to the world.

The fighting which continued to go on throughout Palestine prevented immediate exploration of the cave. Meanwhile, the news of the value of the scrolls circulated among the Bedouin tribes, who at once looted the caves indiscriminately and put on the market every fragment they found. In 1949, however, G. Lankester Harding, Chief Inspector of Antiquities in Jordan, and Father Roland de Vaux, head of the French Dominican School of Archaeology in Jerusalem, officially took charge of the exploration of all caves. While the goatherds continued their sporadic searches, Harding and Father De Vaux carefully and thoroughly explored the cave where the original finds had been made.

Although they discovered no additional scrolls in the first

Cave No. 4 at the Qumran Caves site in Jordan, near the Dead
Sea, where the discovery of the Dead Sea Scrolls occurred

cave, they did recover many fragments of manuscripts as well
as pottery jars like those the goatherds had first seen. Later
they went on to other caves, finding numerous additional
manuscripts, most of them in fragments, some so tiny that only
single letters or parts of letters were contained on them.

That part of the world which consisted of archaeologists,
biblical scholars, and theologians was soon in an uproar. For the
different manuscripts and fragments included remains of nearly
every book of the Old Testament, perhaps of all, as well as
many commentaries. Most of the scrolls were of parchment,
but a few were of papyrus, and among the later finds were two

rolls of copper, about eleven inches high and eight feet long in all.

In addition to the jars, scrolls, and fragments, the finds included linen textiles, apparently used as scroll wrappers or jar covers, bowls, an urn, and many small pieces of pottery. There were a few leather cases, and portions of a wooden comb.

One additional find was so obvious to the goatherds that they overlooked it entirely. This was a ruined half-buried building, the Khirbet Qumran, on the edge of the valley. Here excavation by Harding and De Vaux uncovered the remains of a table and bench, ink stands, and two pieces of pottery on which the Hebrew alphabet was written. The building had been the home of a Jewish religious sect and the table was probably the very one upon which many of the manuscripts were copied. Nearby were cemeteries in which male skeletons were found, as well as the bones of a few women and children.

Further exploration in other valleys has uncovered manuscripts later than those of the Wadi Qumran and has helped to piece together the story these tell.

The Khirbet Qumran was almost certainly the retreat of a group known as *Essenes,* an ascetic Jewish sect who founded the community about 140 B.C. Like a retreat of the Middle Ages built by warrior monks, the settlement included rooms for preparing and eating food, along with a thick-walled lookout tower. It is doubtful whether the Essenes permitted marriage, for they lived a severe life in which material pleasures were greatly limited, even their meals having the character of solemn religious ceremonies. Individuals who joined the community were baptized, the baptism being repeated at least once a year.

Two thousand years ago Palestine was apparently as disturbed politically as it was when the scrolls were found. The small Jewish kingdom of which the Bible tells had split in two and had then been overrun by various neighbors, including the Babylonians and Assyrians. Later it had been conquered by Egypt, Persia, Syria, and Rome. Frequent revolts against the conquerors and their foreign ways had resulted in severe punishment. We do not know which particular invader the Essenes feared. They did expect an end to the world they knew, and to meditate on the coming destruction as well as to prepare for the world to come, they had withdrawn to the region alongside the Dead Sea.

Under the circumstances, their chief duties were raising food for their frugal meals and copying sacred books. These included not only the Bible but a number of commentaries, and numerous writings of a non-biblical nature, some of them previously known in Greek or other languages, the rest new to scholars. Most of the scrolls were written in Hebrew using an old form of the Hebrew alphabet, but there are remains of about sixty manuscripts written in Aramaic, an old dialect akin to Hebrew.

Once the scrolls had been dug up it became a challenge to unroll them without subjecting them to the fate so commonly reported a hundred years ago by the discoverers of mummies and manuscripts, that "they at once crumbled into dust." Before the different manuscripts themselves were tackled, preliminary experiments were performed with small samples that apparently contained no writing, and methods of treatment were developed. It was found that on exposure to moisture the hard and brittle parchment softened sufficiently for the layers to be separated by careful manipulation with a paper knife. The darkening which had resulted from age could be overcome with a mild bleaching agent. In one case bleaching revealed writing on a fragment which appeared blank.

The technique for opening was thus carefully worked out. The scroll fragments were exposed to moisture, and when sufficiently soft, were transferred to a refrigerator to congeal the black, sticky material which had formed. Now the layers could be separated without damage and the pieces of parchment mounted between glass plates for further study.

Some samples of writing were restored to legibility by bleaching, but most were photographed with infrared light, which revealed details of inscriptions previously impossible to read.

The two copper scrolls were badly corroded, cracked, broken, and covered with a stony layer of mineral dust blown in from the desert. After cleaning with dental equipment they were coated with a synthetic resin to keep the copper from falling apart, baked in an oven, and then separated, each layer of copper being carefully cut with a specially designed circular saw to permit sections to be lifted off without breaking. One copper scroll required a week to unroll, and the sections obtained were all photographed, both the photographs and the original copper being used for translation.

The copper scrolls differed in literary content from those of parchment. Whereas the latter were concerned with religious and prophetic writings, the copper contained traditional tales about the hiding places of ancient treasures, mostly gold and silver which together totaled almost two hundred tons. Most of the treasures were supposedly in the neighborhood of Jerusalem and some archaeologists have doubted their existence. But it must be recalled that archaeologists have doubted the existence of other treasures described in ancient documents and that such treasures have later been found.

In the meantime, on the advice of Dr. Millar Burrows, an American archaeologist of the Yale Divinity School, the Metropolitan Samuel came to America, where he sold his scrolls for $250,000. The purchaser, through an intermediary, was the State of Israel.

After a number of scrolls had been unrolled and their contents studied, new problems arose. Were the scrolls as ancient as they seemed, or were they forgeries, possibly old forgeries? One professor of rabbinical literature hinted that the scrolls were placed in the cave to be found, and that they dated from the seventh century A.D., when they were written by "ignorant people"—ignorant people who were so intelligent that they presumably foresaw the founding of a science of archaeology some twelve hundred years later.

What evidence is there of the time when the scrolls were actually written? It is of several kinds. First of all are the archaeological finds obtained by excavation—the presence of Roman coins, household utensils, the plan of the ruined building, the skeletons in the graveyard. Then there are the nature of the writing and of the ancient script, as well as of the text itself. And finally there is the evidence of radiocarbon dating, which gives an age of approximately two thousand years and is supported by all the other evidence available.

Modern scientific methods have played a large part in the investigation of the scrolls. Many of the letters and words in different manuscripts are defaced or lost, and the scholar engaged in studying them is faced with the task of filling in what is missing. In view of the strong feelings aroused in many learned men whose theories conflict it is possible that even scholarly guesses about missing portions may be influenced by prejudice. At this point, therefore, an electronic computer has been allowed to take over. The texts of published scrolls have been put on cards and processed by machine so that the frequency, use, and sequence of words in a given context are tabulated. The result gives an unprejudiced mathematical analysis of a scroll author's "style," and permits the filling in of gaps according to the probabilities of that same style. The machine has been tested by leaving out words intentionally, and it has filled in a gap of as many as five consecutive words without a mistake.

Other archaeological evidence has been supplied by a study of the pottery and the linen textiles. Examination has revealed the method of spinning of the thread as well as its fineness, quality, and method of weaving. Even such matters as the nature of the blue color used in decoration and the technical details which relate the cloth to the methods of spinning and weaving used by other peoples who lived about the same time have been studied. All the observations made on the linen, including radiocarbon measurements, are compatible with a date toward the end of the first century A.D., which is also the date suggested by coins found at the settlement of Khirbet Qumran.

In the face of such a mass of evidence, the suspicions expressed by our professor of rabbinical literature seem farfetched. Skepticism may be justified with regard to the word of two goatherds who may or may not have been part-time smugglers. It appears absurd in face of the excavations carried out by such men as Harding and De Vaux. And it makes no sense whatever when we take into account not only the evidence of the scrolls themselves but all the supporting evidence of pottery, coins, scroll fragments, skeletons in the cemetery, carbon dating, and so on.

Why are tempers so hot when the question of the Dead Sea Scrolls is debated, why are accusations of forgery made on such flimsy evidence, why do some individuals hail the discovery as tremendously significant and others play it down as interesting but not really of first-rate importance? Specialists in different fields of archaeology of course have much to learn from the scrolls about such subjects as the grammar of the ancient Hebrew and Aramaic languages and the history of the alphabet. Students of biblical criticism have obtained new texts which can be compared with the texts previously available and can shed light on details hitherto obscure. But such subjects as these do not usually cause tempers to flare.

The widespread excitement about the scrolls arises from the fact that they deal with a very intensely personal subject concerning which most individuals have strong emotional reactions—religion. Now archaeology has always been much concerned with religion. So long, however, as its studies dealt with the superstitions of primitive man or the long-dead systems of ancient Egypt or Sumeria, so long as the information it turned up concerned gods like Isis and Horus and Enlil and Marduk, no emotions were aroused. But the religions so vividly illuminated by the Dead Sea Scrolls are Judaism and Christianity, both of them very much alive today, both having the support of millions of adherents. Hence every major discovery involving the scrolls and every interpretation of every such discovery has aroused violent debate.

One of the scrolls tells of the coming "War of the Sons of Light with the Sons of Darkness." Another gives a Manual of Discipline for the Essene community itself. A third, which contains a Commentary on Habakkuk, one of the books of the Old Testament, tells of the struggle between a Righteous Teacher and a Wicked Priest. Scattered through these accounts are parallels with stories of the New Testament. Is this to be the story of Utnapishtim and Noah all over again? Was the New Testament partly derived from such previously written manuscripts? Scholars who believe that it was emphasize the parallelism and discover it where some of their colleagues assert that this parallelism does not exist. Many of these scholars on different sides of the fence, it must be emphasized, have religious affiliations with schools of divinity of the Jewish or Christian religion. In interpreting the significance and value of the scrolls they cannot help being influenced by their own religious beliefs.

Thus, although there is fairly general agreement that the scrolls are authentic and date back to 200 B.C. or possibly 68 A.D., and that they do refer to the Essenes, there is fairly general disagreement about the light cast on the early history of Christianity, on the relation between the early Christians and the Jewish sects of the period, and on the meaning of the scrolls for religion.

Perhaps it should be noted that these aspects of the subject, which arouse so much passion in theologians and individuals intensely conscious of their religion, have only a minor interest for archaeology proper. Nevertheless, archaeologists cannot entirely remove themselves from the controversy. As expert witnesses, they have been called upon by both sides. They must testify, however, as scientists and not as partisans of one religious group or another, and their approach must be first to secure as much genuine and pertinent evidence as possible and second to interpret this evidence objectively, with as little prejudice as possible. Willy-nilly, they are involved in the hornet's nest of controversy which the discovery of the Dead Sea Scrolls has stirred up. But with the proper scientific approach they may avoid being stung.

XIII - THE RICHES OF INDIA

When Alexander the Great invaded India in 327 b.c., he found a rich and flourishing civilization. He noted the splendor of cities and princely palaces and was impressed by the advanced state of many arts and crafts. He fought against elephants in battle and marveled at their widespread employment in peaceful pursuits. But the conqueror of the Persian Empire was accustomed to marvels, and to him and his followers the people of India were merely prosperous barbarians, far behind the Greeks in cultural attainments. He attempted to introduce features of Greek civilization, then already approaching the end of its greatest period, but in this he was largely unsuccessful. After he left India, his name was never forgotten and survived in folklore and legend.

The Western world's impressions of India were for many centuries colored by the memory of what Alexander's scribes and historians reported. In the early part of the nineteenth century, new colors were added to the picture. It was found that India had been invaded about a thousand years before Alexander by a people who spoke an Indo-European or "Aryan" language, and were themselves therefore called "Aryans." The invaders were supposed to have brought civilization to a backward country.

Later in the nineteenth century, Bruce Foote, a British geologist, inspired by the discoveries of Paleolithic artifacts in Europe, went looking for similar stone tools in south India. In 1863 and later he discovered the first specimens of what eventually became a large collection, indicating that primitive man had lived in the vast country for countless generations. Had this primitive man developed as his fellows had in Europe and Africa? No immediate answer could be given. But in 1873, a British general and archaeologist, Sir Alexander Cunningham, excavated at Harappa, in the western Punjab, some three hundred miles from Delhi. Here he found pottery, and a stone seal engraved with picture symbols. The presence of this seal, whose characters appeared to be an early form of a script used in the fourth century B.C., suggested the existence of an ancient civilization. But this civilization was not related to any other then known, and the excavations were not carried very far. They were in fact discontinued for almost fifty years.

In 1921, the Indian archaeologist Daya Ram Sahni began new excavations of several mounds at Harappa, and discovered that the civilization represented there was prehistoric. Meanwhile, at Mohenjo-daro, four hundred miles away in the prov-

Deep excavations at Harappa showing the height of the ancient structures

ince of Sind, the attention of Rakhal Das Banerji, Superintendent of Archaeological Survey in the area, was attracted to what appeared to be Buddhist remains. Mohenjo-daro lies not far from Karachi in what is now Pakistan, and the name means "Mound of the Killed." Banerji hoped to discover old shrines of interest to students of Buddhism and, if he was lucky, twelve stone pillars with Indian and Greek inscriptions that dated from the time of Alexander.

[167]

He was luckier than he had dared hope. In his digging he soon discovered thirty cells of an old shrine, arranged around what had been a courtyard. A number of coins found in the ruins identified the time of the shrine as that of an Indian king. Then, as Banerji dug deeper, he came across several seals which resembled the one found at Harappa.

When the finds at Mohenjo-daro came to the attention of Sir John Marshall, Director-General of Archaeology in India, he perceived the striking resemblance to the finds at Harappa and made a careful comparison of seals, pottery, and other material that had been uncovered. In 1924 he announced that the sites represented essentially the same culture, and in *The Illustrated London News* described the two cities as being Indian Tiryns and Mycenae.

Actually, the Indian cities corresponded to cultures even more ancient than those discovered by Schliemann. Other Indian archaeologists continued to dig at Mohenjo-daro where Banerji left off, and in 1925 and 1926, Sir John Marshall took charge, assisted by both British and Indian archaeologists. Work there continued under various excavators through a good part of 1931.

During the period from 1927-1931, other archaeologists had been exploring different parts of Sind, as well as Baluchistan, to the west. A number of villages were found, along with a small town and an early fortress, and some of these were studied more thoroughly in the following years. Additional finds were made south of Sind, so that by the time World War II broke out, the area over which the Indus civilization extended was known to have been much greater than the area of civilized Egypt or Sumeria.

During and immediately after the war, Prof. R. E. Mortimer Wheeler restudied both sites with more advanced scientific methods and traced a relation between the Indus civilization and the later Indian civilizations of written history.

The evidence as a whole shows that the Indus Valley was, like early Egypt and Sumeria, the home of a Chalcolithic or "Copper-Stone" civilization. That is, the use of copper and bronze was known, but the metal was so difficult to obtain and work that most implements were made of stone. Different investigators have ascribed different dates, but Mohenjo-daro and Harappa appear to have existed as far back as 2300 B.C.

In both cities the houses were finely built for people accustomed to luxurious living, as shown by the existence of wells, drains, and bathrooms. Weapons were made of stone, as well as copper and bronze, and skilled artisans worked with gold, silver, copper, and ivory. The making of pottery was well ad-

Detailed view of an ancient well at Mohenjo-daro

[169]

vanced, and, very likely, the art of sculpture also. Cotton was used for textiles here long before its value was discovered in Egypt and Mesopotamia.

Many plants and animals had been domesticated, the former including wheat, barley, rice, and dates in addition to cotton, the latter including cattle, buffalo, sheep, pigs, chickens, dogs, elephants, and camels. The pictographic form of writing developed in the Indus Valley was quite different from either hieroglyphic or cuneiform scripts.

The high degree of development and the uniformity of the Indus Valley civilization over so wide an area are of great significance. It had so definite a stamp of its own that even today, thousands of years later, we can recognize some of its traits. The modern inhabitants of India possess skills and follow customs in many ways like those of the ancient dwellers along the Indus.

Did these early civilizations develop without help from the outside? Evidence has been found that the cities of the Indus Valley traded with the Sumerians of the same period. Danish archaeologists have investigated the island of Bahrein, a small piece of land (thirty miles long at most by ten miles wide) on the Persian Gulf. Until the middle of the twentieth century, no important ruins had been found here. It had been known that Bahrein contained a vast number of burial mounds, at least a hundred thousand, but the island had been considered only a cemetery, of no great importance otherwise. Other archaeologists had studied a few of the tombs. The Danish expedition, however, searched for the town in which the people who had built the tombs lived. Over a period of five years the group not only discovered the ancient town itself, but found enough artifacts to show that the site had been continuously occupied for about five thousand years. Among the objects discovered were five seals showing warriors in helmets of Sumerian type. Similar seals have been found in the Indus Valley, and the evidence indicates clearly that Bahrein was a trading center linking the two civilizations.

Investigators have of course asked: which civilization came first? Did these early inhabitants of India owe their progress from barbarism to the civilizing influence of the Sumerians, or was it the other way around? Or did both civilizations arise separately?

Most archaeologists continue to give priority to the Sumerians. But the final answer appears to be hidden below soil still waiting to be dug. For many reasons, the evidence needed to make a decision has been delayed. Even before World War II, many of the buildings at Mohenjo-daro, exposed to the air after thousands of years of burial, began to deteriorate. Excavators know that often their work of discovery destroys valuable finds. Usually they try to extract the utmost information possible before old buildings and walls crumble into fragments. At Mohenjo-daro, lack of money and lack of interest from those in power permitted destruction to go too far too soon.

In one respect, however, the evidence is enough to show a decisive difference between the Indus civilization and the contemporary civilizations of Egypt and Mesopotamia. Religion played a part in Indian daily life, but did not dominate it. The Egyptians built their greatest buildings, the pyramids, as homes for dead kings and queens, the Sumerians their greatest, the ziggurats, as temples for the glory of gods. With all this labor for the benefit of royal or supernatural beings, there was little left for the ordinary Egyptian or Sumerian, who lived wretchedly. The Indus Valley inhabitants built for themselves. "The finest structures," says Marshall, "are those erected for the convenience of the citizens."

It is worthy of ironical note that India, which most of us think of as concerned with mysticism and affairs of the spirit, in contrast to the materialistic interests of the West, was at this early stage in history intelligently concerned with the material welfare of its citizens, in contrast to the gloomy spiritual interests of the Asian and African civilizations of its own time and of the Incan, Mayan, and Asian civilizations which came later.

Much more work is needed on the ancient cities of the Indus Valley before we can establish their relation to Egypt and Sumeria. So much of the area is unexplored that every few years we can expect another shock of discovery. Meanwhile, archaeologists are working to construct a chronological table of events in India. Starting with the Paleolithic, and progressing through the Neolithic and Chalcolithic Eras, they are investigating the transitional stages into the period of written history. Only then will it be possible to determine accurately what the present world owes to the Indus civilizations of the past.

XIV · ARCHAEOLOGY
THE WORLD OVER

THE DISCOVERY OF A NEANDERTHAL SKELETON IN 1856 AND THE
publication three years later of Darwin's *The Origin of Species*
aroused great interest in man's distant past, extending back to
the time when he became man. While argument still went on
as to whether Neanderthal Man was a predecessor of *Homo
sapiens* or merely a deformed specimen of the latter, a new find
contributed to the increase of excitement. In 1868 workmen
digging a roadbed for a railroad discovered in a locality of
France called Cro-Magnon a number of flints and animal bones
which dated back to the late Old Stone or Upper Paleolithic

[173]

Era. Archaeologists were called in, and at Cro-Magnon, Louis Lartet uncovered five human skeletons which turned out to be of modern type. It was not long before the Cro-Magnon skeletons were as famous as their Neanderthal predecessor.

The archaeological search for man's ancestors was now going on all over Europe. Human antiquity was established beyond doubt, but the manner in which human characteristics had evolved, both physically and socially, was still completely unknown. Was Neanderthal Man a creature intermediate between the true apes and *Homo sapiens*? He was certainly a man of some kind, although he had apelike features. He had developed the skill to create flint and bone tools, a skill which was passed on in human fashion from one generation to the next, and in many ways he lived like a man, rather than an ape.

If he was human, however, what was his relation to the completely modern Cro-Magnon Man? Surely the differences between them were too great for one species to have evolved into the other.

As time went on, evidence accumulated of early man's interest in matters beyond the ken of any ape. Remains were found of burial accompanied by primitive religious rites, and occasional carvings on bones indicated an early interest in "art." And then, in 1879, a discovery was made that revolutionized all ideas of man's direct ancestors.

For some years the Marquis de Sautuola had been investigating the great cave of Altamira, in northern Spain. He had made a number of finds which were of interest, but not of great importance. Then, one day in 1879, when he set out for the cave, he took with him a companion—his daughter, aged twelve, who was tired of being left at home day after day. It was this little girl who made the great discovery.

In low-ceilinged passages and chambers where a grown man had either to crawl or to walk bent over, with eyes on the ground, a child could walk upright, and even raise her head. The little girl raised her head, and gaped in astonishment. Soon she came running to her father. "Papa, Papa," she cried, "look, painted bulls!"

The Marquis looked. Above his head were the works of the first great forerunners of Michelangelo and Picasso. All over the ceiling of the cave were paintings of animals, among them bison, which his daughter had taken for bulls. Standing out boldly over bumpy areas, shadowed in the depressions, the beasts formed a three-dimensional panorama of the Paleolithic Era that stretched as far as his dim lamp let him see. Created by a combination of engraving and painting with pigments, the figures startled him by their artistic genius.

A prehistoric painting of a crouching bison found in the cave at Altamira, Spain

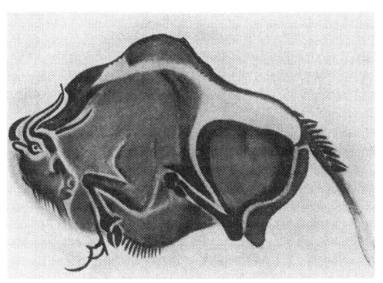

When De Sautuola reported his discovery, however, the usual first reaction prevailed. The paintings were denounced by many scholars as frauds. The Marquis, it was declared, had hired a wandering artist to crawl into the cave, and under the most inconvenient circumstances an artist would be likely to encounter, presumably by the flickering light of tallow candles, using a technique completely foreign to modern painters, to spend months creating paintings of animals so long extinct that neither the artist nor the Marquis had ever seen them!

The skepticism of some of these critics is worth noting. After the episode with the workmen of Boucher de Perthes, not long before, they had every right to suspect fraud. They had no right to be convinced of it. The paintings themselves were breathtakingly beautiful and have since been hailed as great works by artists and critics alike. That an unknown painter of the nineteenth century could have created them was incredible. And all the evidence, including the nature of the technique used, the chemical composition of the pigments, and other finds made in the cave, suggested that they were genuine. To make the cries of fraud seem more absurd, other drawings had been found a year before in a French cave, and although these were of lesser quality, the circumstances of the discovery made it clear that the work was of great age. But the skeptics had made up their minds: Paleolithic Man was no artist, and any one who found his paintings was a fraud!

He may have been no artist most of the time, but in the next few years other examples of his skill in painting and engraving kept cropping up, particularly in French caves, and under such circumstances that there could be no question of authenticity. Soon the critics began to eat their words, and the genuineness of Paleolithic Cave Art was established.

Meanwhile, other skeletons of both Neanderthal Man and

Homo sapiens were being found. Both species may have existed side by side, possibly as far back as a hundred thousand years ago. Even earlier species of apelike men were being found not only in Europe but in Asia, although the question of how the different types were related, difficult enough at best, was confused by the Piltdown forgery. But in the past few years a great deal of new evidence has been produced which has settled a few of the disputed points.

For one thing, it appears that Cro-Magnon and Neanderthal Man arose separately. It has recently become evident that there were two types of the latter, the "classic" Neanderthal, which was more apelike, and the "progressive," some of whom may have been a hybrid of Neanderthal and *Homo sapiens*. Both types appear to have died out about forty thousand years ago, very possibly killed off by their Cro-Magnon rivals. Before Neanderthal Man disappeared he had developed a culture, called Mousterian, which was at least as advanced as that of our apparently direct ancestors.

As new sites for excavation were found, better methods of studying them were evolved. In Asia Minor and Mesopotamia, Austrian and German archaeologists were perfecting methods of digging up the famous *tells,* or mounds. And in England, General Lane Fox Pitt-Rivers was developing new techniques of both digging and recording. With sufficient money to hire all the men he needed and to publish his results, and more important, with the intelligence to use his money wisely, Pitt-Rivers began to excavate total sites. This was of course possible only if the total site was not too large. He appreciated the importance of stratigraphic digging—that is, the removal of one layer of soil at a time—and, unlike most of the archaeologists up to his time, he had the imagination and forethought to realize that other investigators would follow him. When he removed an entire barrow at Handley Downs, he left four pillars that would permit his successors to note the height of the barrow and examine the different strata for themselves.

In some cases, he removed entire barrows and then built them up again to their previous size. But in each of these cases, he had an account of his excavation engraved on a sheet of lead, which was buried for the information of later archaeologists. It need hardly be said that a man who took such pains dug with great care, and made tremendous numbers of drawings, architects' plans, sections, and models. In addition, he preserved everything he found. The techniques which he and other great archaeologists worked out have been the basis for the advanced methods of study now in use.

The origin of the modern human species is only one of the great problems to which scholars with anthropological training devote considerable attention. In almost every field of regional archaeology—in England, the European mainland, Crete, Egypt, Asia Minor, China, India, Mexico, or Peru—as events are traced back, excavators find themselves studying more and more primitive cultures. But the relations between cultures of five or twenty thousand years ago cannot be understood on a local basis. Scholars interested in early man must have more than regional interests.

Important finds occur everywhere. On Santa Rosa, an island off the California Coast, the dating of shells from a deep deposit suggests that man lived here more than thirty thousand years ago. Finds in other places suggest that man was in the New World more than twenty thousand years ago. We must await the discovery, excavation, and dating of more sites before the story of early man in the Americas can be worked out in detail.

All over the world, mysteries have turned up to set archaeol-

ogists against each other. One of the most interesting involves
Easter Island, a lonely, rocky piece of irregularly shaped land
about eight miles wide at its widest by fifteen miles in length,
lost in the vast area of the Pacific between Asia and the west
coast of South America. Since Easter Day in 1722, when it was
discovered, the island has aroused interest and curiosity. On
this small spot, the first Europeans found to their amazement
a number of great stone statues, some thirty feet or more high.
Who had carved these statues, who had moved the tons of stone
into position? The people who then inhabited the island appeared incapable of such feats. But if not they, who else?

Archaeologists generally have believed that the island was
colonized by Polynesians from other islands, such as the Mar-
quesas and Mangareva, further west, about the fourteenth or
fifteenth century. Inscriptions on so-called "talking boards"
found on the island have recently been translated and shown
to be in a language like that spoken by other Polynesian groups.
Evidence of this kind has been used against a theory that
Easter Island was colonized from America.

But this evidence proves nothing, says the proponent of
colonization from America. An expedition led by Thor Heyerdahl did considerable excavation on Easter Island, explored
secret caves, and uncovered much new evidence, including
buried statues of a new type. Heyerdahl agrees that immigrants
did arrive from the Western Pacific. But he thinks they came
late. Dates from radioactive carbon in western Polynesia are
few. Those obtained indicate occupation back to about 900
A.D. Dates from Easter Island, on the other hand, show that
men were present there by the end of the fourth century. Moreover, it is the only settlement in the Pacific where evidence has
been found of the masonry technique used in Peru. Heyerdahl
thinks the early statues on Easter Island resemble the pre-

Stone statues on Easter Island

Incan statues of Peru. Such Peruvian plants as sweet potatoes and totora reeds point toward South America, too. The early architects of Easter Island oriented some of their religious structures by the sun, as did the ancient Peruvians. As a crowning piece of evidence, Heyerdahl reports that the Easter Islanders, in blood type, are related to the American Indians, not to the Southeast Asians, although their language is grouped along with that of the Malays. In his opinion, this indicates early colonization by pre-Incan peoples of America, followed much later by colonization from the direction of Asia. Later work by others, however, indicates that the blood-type evidence is inconclusive.

Let us leave the Pacific and skip over the surface of the globe to the Atlantic Coast. Off Denmark, several hundred frogmen have been exploring under water and finding new settlements that date as far back as 4000 B.C. Thousands of flints, arrowheads, and fragments of pottery have already come to light. As frogmen outnumber archaeologists by perhaps a hundred to one, and as it takes a moment to find a piece of pottery and possibly days or weeks to study it, we can see that Danish archaeologists have plenty of material to work with. How Thomsen and Nillson and Worsaae would have enjoyed helping in the classification of these old relics, now being studied at the same National Museum in Copenhagen where they themselves worked!

Enough additional sites are known in Asia and Africa, let alone Europe or the Western Hemisphere, to keep students of ancient cultures busy for the next hundred years. And there are vast portions of the earth's surface that have never been touched by the archaeologist's spade. People once lived in what are now jungles or deserts, not to speak of lands like those of ancient Denmark, now sunk beneath the sea. Some day these jungles and deserts and drowned lands will be investigated, and will yield discoveries to surprise the coming generations as the work of Botta and Layard and Schliemann and Petrie surprised the past.

Even now, a few individuals maintain that we are completely mistaken in our ideas of where civilization arose. They point to Abyssinia or Central Africa as worthy of exploration, and until these areas are thoroughly excavated, who can say that they are wrong?

It is clear that despite what yet remains to be done, archaeology has advanced far during the past century. Its entire approach has changed. No longer is interest limited to the problems of one ancient people or one area. Today's emphasis is on the relations of different peoples, on attempts to chart their movements, the contacts between them, the transmission of cultural traits from one to another. These are important and difficult problems, and when we consider the short period during which a small number of men and women have been at work on them, the progress made appears amazing.

Let us examine a bit more closely the kinds of men and women who have accomplished so much.

XV - THE TRAINING
OF AN ARCHAEOLOGIST

IF YOU ARE INTERESTED IN ARCHAEOLOGY AS A HOBBY, IF YOU would like to devote your spare time to helping uncover the life of the past without hoping to make a living by your activities, you can be extremely useful and happy at the same time. In many excavations in the United States and Great Britain, for instance, professionals and amateurs work together to their mutual benefit. The professional obtains the services of a devoted individual spurred on by an interest in what he is doing. The amateur receives the necessary guidance and direction in his work, and enjoys a combination of physical and mental labor which can be highly satisfying.

Amateurs who dig alone run into trouble. There are exceptions to this rule, of course, as to almost all rules, but lacking professional training, few people know how to dig properly or how to interpret their finds, and without such knowledge digging is merely destruction. The spade of the ignorant, though it may uncover wonderful witnesses of the past, usually destroys them before they can give their evidence to intelligent judges. For such clumsy excavators archaeologists have always had a strong dislike.

If you want to work as an amateur, it would be a good idea to read and subscribe to such journals as *Antiquity, American Antiquity,* and *Archaeology.* You can secure from them or other sources the names and addresses of local archaeological groups, take part in their activities, and in time become a most useful and respected colleague.

What should you learn? That depends on your interests. If you work with professionals who have all-round training, you will suffer less from the gaps in your own knowledge. And such gaps will be inevitable. Even such a brilliant man as Schliemann, the excavator of ancient Troy, for all his brilliance made serious mistakes, and eventually found it desirable to hire a professionally trained assistant. And there is a great deal more to learn in archaeology than there was in his nineteenth-century day.

Many of the great archaeologists of the past were essentially self-taught in archaeology, whatever their formal education in other fields. Schliemann, Thomsen, Champollion, and Stephens could not learn their archaeology at school, for there were no schools where it was taught. The situation has changed in the last century. The archaeology of prehistoric man and of primitive peoples all over the world is taught in the United States under Anthropology, the study of man. An amateur who is interested in the archaeology of the American Indian, including the high cultures of Middle and South America, should consult with a member of the Department of Anthropology at the university nearest his home. The archaeology of Greece and Rome may be taught under the heading of History of Art, Ancient History, or Latin and Greek. That of the Near East is most likely to be included in Ancient History. Museums vary greatly in their interests and may have on their staffs one or more archaeologists concerned with different branches of archaeology. The best opportunity for the amateur in the United States is to be found in cooperating with anthropologists in the unraveling of the prehistory of the New World. To assist an archaeologist in his research, it is usually unnecessary to register for courses at a university.

Despite all difficulties, young men and women do enter the profession, but not in great numbers. In the world as a whole, there are and always have been few professional archaeologists, and the great discoveries made over the course of the past two centuries have been the work of a few men and a handful of women.

If like these few you do enter the profession, what are the satisfactions you can hope to achieve? They are numerous and varied. The thrill of discovery, of bringing to life people and events long dead and forgotten, of solving riddles of incredible difficulty can be yours. It is a thrill difficult to match. Moreover, as an archaeologist you can live a life of excitement in the field, often spiced with danger, alternating with peaceful study in a library or museum.

You will usually end up as a specialist in some geographical area. You have the whole world to choose from—Peru, Brazil, Mesopotamia, Egypt, Alaska, Norway, or Iran, for example. At the same time you will become a jack-of-all-trades which involve a knowledge of human nature. If you expect to be a field archaeologist you must learn how to persuade wealthy and influential people, or research foundations, to pay the expenses of an expedition. You must be able to organize and direct the expedition after you have the money, as well as to interpret your findings after you obtain them.

You must possess, in addition to an awareness of what scientific methods can do, an expert's understanding of your own specialty. And you must learn a great deal about the arts and crafts. All this learning presupposes a love of study, and even a lifetime of it will not be enough unless you are quick to learn.

To be a successful archaeologist you had better aim for your goal as early as possible—as far back as secondary school, if you are one of the rare individuals who know their minds at that primitive stage. By beginning in your teens you can more easily adjust to the prospect of learning how to handle money, people, and ideas, and at the same time give up the hope of attaining wealth yourself. You can start learning how to write and speak fluently in English, and how to translate from different languages, including French, German, Latin, and Greek, if you are interested in the classical world, or Spanish, if you plan to work in Central or South America.

You had better, in fact, become accustomed to the idea of picking up a new language as readily as a chemist or biologist learns a new technique that has suddenly become important. Actually, acquiring command of a language is not frighteningly difficult for a talented boy or girl with a reasonable amount of determination. In preparation for his excavations at Troy, Schliemann picked up almost a score of new languages in the intervals of an extremely busy life. Champollion, preparing to translate the mysterious hieroglyphics, learned not only a number of ancient tongues, but Coptic, or modern Egyptian, and Arabian, Syrian, Parsi, and Chinese as well, knowing that any one of these might give him a clue to the pattern of the ancient script. Study grammar with half a mind, as most students do in the average school room, and you will be able after three years to manage a crude French or German equivalent of "How do you do, Mr. Smith? Is your aunt in the garden?" Approach a language with the enthusiasm of an apprentice mastering a form of sorcery that will open doors to worlds now locked, and you can learn it reasonably well in three to six months.

While you are absorbing new languages, you had also better be studying the history of art and acquiring a mastery of both free hand and mechanical drawing. You should also learn to type, for you will spend a great deal of time writing reports, and you must learn photography in order to illustrate your finds. Such skills, acquired in youth, will be useful for a lifetime. Along with art you had better study architecture and surveying, and if possible a little civil engineering. Sir Flinders Petrie, a great Egyptologist, insisted that a knowledge of engineering was as important to an archaeologist as a knowledge of ancient art. You can profitably spend spare moments (if you can find them) watching workmen put up houses, construct highways, and build bridges. A knowledge of practical methods may come in handy when you try to reconstruct the ways in which Bronze Age carpenters or stone masons worked.

You must become proficient in a broad field such as anthropology or ancient history, for it is in these fields that archaeological problems occur. You may be under the impression that geography is a subject for grammar school students only. But in college you will find it necessary to restudy geography completely from an adult point of view.

All this comes under the heading of general education for the pursuit of an archaeological career, and you will get similar advice from many professionals already in the field. It may differ, however, in emphasis. Historically, archaeology was rooted in the study of the humanities, beginning with classical art and gradually broadening its scope to include Egyptian and ancient Near Eastern art. The translation of newly found languages, another field of great humanistic interest, has played a major role in it. And the archaeologist has been able to regard himself as a historian and scientist as well.

It is difficult to change old habits of thought. But some archaeologists, like the rest of us, have underestimated the importance of science. Do not, of course, neglect the humanities, but don't fail to make science an important part of your training. Get a good grounding in fundamentals, and keep an eye out for scientific advances.

While continuing this generalized training—and you can see what a background of information it requires—you can begin, perhaps in the latter half of your college career, to specialize. You may not even have to make a conscious choice, for your specialty will be a subject that has aroused your spontaneous interest. But better not try to carry specialization too far at first, as you can continue this phase of your training in graduate school—if you are lucky enough to find and be accepted in one that gives the courses you want.

Even the largest universities cannot give courses in more than a few specialties, and these are subject to change as professors retire or shift their academic allegiance, and new men take their places. This means that you may have to shop around by mail or in person for the graduate school you want to attend and then persuade it to accept you. This too is part of your training in learning how to handle people in your study of the obsolescent customs of different civilizations.

Under the best of circumstances, classroom instruction or study with a small group in graduate school will not make you an archaeologist. You must learn to dig, and you can start by working with local and state archaeological societies where you live or study. And then you must learn to use your mind on your own. Such use implies the ability to disagree—intelligently, however, and not out of sheer ignorance or contrariness—with what the most distinguished teachers of archaeology will tell you. When you have reached that stage you are ready for an archaeological position of your own—if you can find one.

There are indications that the entire situation in education and science is changing, and there are hopes that the change will be for the better. In the future you may therefore be able to become an archaeologist somewhat more easily, without having to overcome obstacles other than those inherent in the subject itself. In some countries, national governments subsidize archaeological research. Our own government hires only a few individuals in this field, but may be induced to hire more and provide money for universities, once the public realizes the importance of the subject. At present, admittedly, this is more hope than reality.

Nevertheless, the public *has* shown great interest in important archaeological discoveries. It has been fascinated by dazzling revelations of the past made by Champollion, Schliemann, Flinders Petrie, Arthur Evans, and other great men. And it is becoming more and more interested in learning how their work is done.

XVI-
AN EXPEDITION PREPARES

LET US ASSUME THAT YOU ARE THE PROSPECTIVE HEAD OF AN EXPE-
dition, anxious to get started as soon as possible at the actual
digging. You have a perspective of the entire scope of archaeology, and have already chosen your main field of interest—
Central America, Italy, Greece, or Mesopotamia. But all of
these are large areas. How do you narrow the field, where
and how do you begin to dig?

That depends on what archaeological riddles you are trying
to solve. In some cases you can save considerable time and
energy by returning to an old site which has not been completely explored. Among these are Pompeii, some of the Mayan
cities of Central America, many of the Mesopotamian tells, and
a number of excavations in both hemispheres ranging from
the ancient cities of Mexico to the Indus Valley and Cambodia.
If you are interested in Paleolithic Man, for instance, you can
find throughout the world various caves where men are known
to have lived and left remains as yet investigated in only a
superficial way.

Wherever you intend to dig, you must first obtain permis-
sion of the government involved. Many countries whose ar-

chaeological wealth has been plundered in the past have now set up rigid regulations which must be carefully followed before they will permit further work. Most governments now insist on the right to keep valuable finds, leaving the excavator himself only his photographs or fragments of bone and pottery. Unfortunate archaeologists who have disregarded these regulations, or been accused of disregarding them, have been jailed and fined.

If you want to start from scratch in a new area, and have complied with government regulations, you can begin with a large-scale aerial survey. In Mesopotamia, mounds indicate the

An aerial survey of the Kimbito Arroya in New Mexico. This type of photography is carefully scanned for mounds by archaeologists

size and shape of buried cities and villages, and fragments of pottery found on the surface sometimes reveal which mounds are most likely to yield useful material. In Ohio or Kansas, if you are interested in the prehistory of the American Indian, mounds and fragments of flint and pottery are likewise useful. If your interest lies in the Old Stone Age, you should survey areas where large caves abound, neglecting flat valleys and concentrating on regions where surface or underground water has eroded steep banks or cliffs.

Many accidental clues can set you on the right path. If peasants in a certain area are using ancient baked bricks for their buildings, those bricks may have come from a long-ruined city. Weigh carefully the reports of farmers who have picked up arrowheads or run across old stone walls while plowing. And occasionally, when an artificial lake or dam is being constructed or a power station is being built, old artifacts can be collected with a minimum of effort. In the United States a small. number of engineering firms have cooperated with archaeological groups, and in Russia archaeological expeditions are often sent to the scene of large-scale industrial and engineering excavations.

Once you have selected your site, you face a difficult executive problem. You may list the things you would like to find, but you have no certainty that you will actually find them. A huge mound may take the work of a hundred men for five years to excavate with reasonable thoroughness. If you cannot hire more than fifty men nor work for more than a year, how much should you plan to dig? Your money will have to be spent carefully, and you may not turn up useful finds for a long time. What plan of excavation should you follow?

You had better have *some* plan or you may work for a year with no results to show, and then you will stand no chance of getting money for a later expedition. On the other hand, your plan should not be too rigid. During the very first week an exciting discovery may change all your ideas, and force you to change the entire direction of your work.

In view of this necessity for both planning and flexibility, how much money will you need? If you ask for too much you may not get it; in fact you may frighten your possible sponsors so badly that they will give you nothing at all. If you ask for too little, of course, you may also be refused on the ground that nothing of any importance can be accomplished with so small a sum. If you do manage to get a small amount you may discover to your chagrin that your money has run out just when your discoveries begin to be interesting.

The financial aspect of the problem is usually the single chief obstacle to archaeological work. Schliemann and Pitt-Rivers were in the unusual position of being financially independent, and not having to count every penny they spent. Few archaeologists are so fortunate. They must depend on sponsorship by universities, museums, and foundations, very often on joint efforts by two or three groups. Wealthy individuals may donate money directly to an expedition or establish funds for archaeological research. Whereas in other countries excavation is largely subsidized by the government, here in the United States it often depends on private support.

Once assured of financial backing, you must organize your expeditionary group. In the past it has been possible to do useful excavation with one or two men. For studies with limited objectives a few men will still suffice. But for a large and important mound you will require many specialists, and each must be supplied with equipment. Moreover, a large mound cannot be opened and then left to be ruined by wind and rain. The layers you dig up you destroy. It is your obligation as an archaeologist to make a thorough examination and record while these are still possible.

You will therefore need an engineer and architect, or one man who can function as both. Someone will have to clean, label, and store the objects found and eventually crate them for shipment, and in many cases you will need an expert at repairing and even restoring those dug up in poor condition. As you will take a tremendous number of notes, at least one person should serve as secretary. If you hope to turn up inscriptions in Persian or Akkadian and you yourself do not know these languages well, it is advisable to take along someone who does. The tablets will have to be translated eventually, and if some of them are translated when found, they may afford clues to fur-

Dr. Nelson Glueck measuring the site of part of a settlement at Wadi Arabah

ther digging. For a similar reason, if you expect to turn up many animal bones, flints, or pottery fragments, it is a good idea to have a member of the expedition who can investigate them on the spot. The objects you find in one week may require a year of study later. Nevertheless, you should know their significance as soon as possible.

You will need a photographer to record different portions of the excavation as well as the appearance of individual objects. If you and the members of your team can shift from one job to another, you may get by with a smaller number of individuals. But if you find a wide variety of objects, the more trained people you have the better.

The individuals named so far are specialists. At the scene of excavation itself, you will hire men to do the actual digging. These must be organized in almost military fashion and trained as they work. Each small squad will be responsible to a foreman, and the foreman will be directly responsible to you. Each individual must be taught his own particular job and his interest in doing it properly kept alive. The bonus system, once popular, is now avoided. All too often it leads to the "salting" of a dig with objects from other sources.

Now that you are in charge of a small army, you will remember, with your fellow general, Napoleon, that every army travels on its stomach. You will need a kitchen and a cook, possibly a housekeeper, and in case members of your expedition (or you yourself, for that matter) have brought children along, you may require a nurse.

You will be very unlikely to need a full-time treasurer and paymaster. But someone, in addition to carrying out other duties, must be in charge of funds, paying the men and ordering supplies as needed. It may dismay you to find that such ordinary jobs are not as simple as they sound. The purchase of an extra dozen spades, for instance, may involve important principles. If you order too much equipment you do not use, your money disappears at a horrifying rate. On the other hand, if you fail to order what you need, you waste the time of many people. It is frustrating to have the work of a dozen men held up for lack of an inexpensive item. For this reason it is advisable to have spare parts for all critical pieces of equipment, from camera lenses to automobile spark plugs.

Having taken care of ordinary archaeological requirements, you must consider a few others. In coming years you may be working with colleagues who are on your own professional level but interested less in the lives of Sumerians or Egyptians or Neolithic Danes than in the weather these ancient people experienced, the plants they grew, the animals on which they fed. Or you may be dependent on extremely skilled technicians, men who can use elaborate and complicated instruments. There is no doubt, for instance, that in the future carbon-14 will be determined by at least some expeditions at the very site of excavation.

Paleometeorology, paleobiology, and paleochemistry are infant sciences, but they are important to you, for the more you know about the environment of the people you study the better you will understand the people themselves. In coming years, therefore, some archaeological expeditions may be even larger than they are now, and may emphasize the biological or chemical aspect of investigation, with you, as the professional archaeologist, no longer head of the team, but one of a number of equals.

Meanwhile, most expeditions of the present continue to concentrate on material remains which bear the most direct relation to the lives of ancient peoples. With this in mind, what is the pattern of your actual digging?

After the survey, the areas to be excavated are chosen and cleared. Lines of stakes are driven into the ground and trenches dug along them. The exact location, width, and length of the trenches will depend on the nature of your clues, on what you are seeking, and on the nature of the ground. In good firm soil you may go down fifty feet or more, and you must make sure that the walls of your trenches do not crumble and collapse, for the layers of soil can be distinguished most clearly in the walls. If you are looking for characteristic finds in a large area, you may dig a large number of parallel trenches, and then cross them with other trenches to form a network. Sometimes an area may be so important that in the course of years you may excavate it completely, first digging your network of trenches, and then digging away the squares which represent the meshes of your net.

A method developed for the excavation of prehistoric sites

A view, from the southwest, of Stonehenge in England, one of the most famous of archaeological finds

in Great Britain is to divide each area into a checkerboard of squares ten or twelve feet wide, separated by ridges two or three feet wide. Each square is excavated separately, the ridges being left standing. This method has been applied to Mesopotamian tells, but is much less common than the method of digging trenches. In any case, it is no longer customary to indicate a large area, distribute spades, and say, "Okay, everybody, start digging." Moreover, no matter what the original method of attack, if a trench runs into an important underground wall or monument, for instance, the original plan of attack may be temporarily suspended, and the area around the find carefully dug up.

Within each square the soil is stripped off layer by layer. The diggers must recognize the new layers at once, by the change in color or consistency of the soil, or some other characteristic. A small amount of soil at a time is loosened before clearing, and the faces of the walls kept vertical. Each layer is examined, possibly even sifted, before it is removed, and the objects found are noted and labeled. It is extremely important that the *relationships* of objects be noted. An arrowhead found among the bones of a skeleton has a quite different significance from one found a dozen feet away. Fragments of wood grouped together may have belonged to a single object, which may be reconstructed. Fragments found in *two* groups may indicate that more than one object existed. For the man faced with the task of reconstruction, the difference is that between trying to put the pieces of a jigsaw puzzle together, and trying to fit together the pieces of two or more puzzles mixed indiscriminately. That is one reason why it is so important to note the exact spot where each object was found.

Soil samples may also be taken for a study of pollen count, or for chemical or bacteriological investigation.

If digging uncovers the wall of a building, it should not be continued along the line of a wall but at right angles. An unexcavated area should be left standing near the wall so that the different layers of soil may serve as reference levels.

If an entire mound, such as that used for burial, is to be excavated, leaving only level ground where it once stood, a contour map should first be made. Otherwise, after excavation, it may be impossible to reconstruct the shape of the mound. In general, of course, to dig is to destroy. It is therefore necessary in all cases for records to be as complete as possible. The first survey should locate the site accurately, and this in itself may be difficult in a country which has not been well mapped as a whole. A plan should be made of the entire area under investigation and as digging proceeds, an individual record should be kept of each trench or subdivision created by the walls of structures found beneath the surface, the description of each layer including nature of soil, thickness, and objects found, located according to a geometrical system of rectangular coordinates.

Along with the written record must go a series of photographs which emphasize the actual features revealed by excavation. An unskillfully made photograph will gloss over important aspects of a find and, worse still, suggest by means of shadows or careless lighting features that are not really present. Photography is important not only because it can record with a single click of the camera details that would take pages of notes to describe, but also because it can catch subtle shadings that the eye cannot perceive at the moment or may overlook altogether. Later on the photographs should be studied as carefully as they have been made.

Where formerly archaeologists dug for the sake of the objects they hoped to recover, now they dig chiefly for the record they expect to make. The objects themselves are important to museums and national collections, but once the archaeologist has studied them and exhausted their capacity to tell him of the past, he is willing to surrender them, unless some sudden inspiration arouses the hope of obtaining information previously overlooked.

Not all objects found can be studied at length. In some cases, bones or broken pieces of pottery may be so numerous that it is impossible to examine each one as carefully as the investigator might wish. But most of them are saved for future examination. Overlook, or worse still, discard something of positive value, and the curse of future archaeologists will be heavy upon you. And archaeological imprecations carry more weight these days than do those of Egyptian Pharaohs.

As for the blessings of archaeology and archaeologists—perhaps we had better consider them separately, for they comprise a difficult and much debated subject.

XVII - THE VALUE
OF ARCHAEOLOGY

WHAT DOES ARCHAEOLOGY HAVE TO OFFER THAT IS WORTH ITS cost? Many a successful expedition has returned with not a single object that would arouse the interest of a jeweler or dealer in precious metals. A financial balance for all archaeological expeditions to date would reveal them as unprofitable enterprises, and their losses are continually increasing as their finds occur more and more in rubbish heaps instead of treasure chests.

Archaeologists themselves have often emphasized, correctly, that their discoveries could not be applied industrially, or pay off in dollars and cents. As the statement is repeated, however, it becomes less and less true. Nowadays, archaeology *is* beginning to pay off. Not in enormous dividends, as yet, but in a way that may indicate a possible trend of the future.

In its relations with other sciences, archaeology has begun to have a commercial value. For the other sciences have begun to devote attention to rather slow processes, events which take place not in a few minutes or days in a test tube or laboratory animal, but over hundreds or thousands of years in nature.

And what study is better qualified to supply information of the kind required for such lengths of time than archaeology itself?

Botanists, for example, have long been intrigued by the origin of maize, or corn, the great staple food of the American civilizations. Did our present maize arise from a hybrid plant between two wild grasses known as *teosinte* and *tripsicum,* or did it have a completely different origin? The question is important in many ways. For one thing, the answer can shed light on the hereditary characteristics of the maize plant, and thus lead eventually to improving it, and in this way add millions of dollars each year to the world's corn crop.

Thanks to archaeological and geological research, botanists are beginning to answer the question. They have identified a fossil pollen at least eighty thousand years old as being almost identical in size and shape with modern corn pollen, thus showing that the maize plant existed as such far back in prehistory. Specimens of ancient cultivated corn fifty-six hundred years old have been found by archaeological expeditions and have added additional information. Using these as a guide, botanists have been able to reconstruct the ancient maize plant fairly closely. Botany, genetics, and archaeology have all gained by this study, and sooner or later the world's food supply will also gain by it.

A much more striking example of commercial value is supplied by archaeological studies in Iraq. The soil of modern Iraq, much of which lies between the Tigris and Euphrates rivers, is largely sterile and poverty-stricken. Ancient Mesopotamia, on the other hand, lying between these same rivers, was famous for its fertility. Part of the difference lies in the change of social conditions of the people over many centuries.

Ancient irrigation systems were neglected and fell into decay, and without water the soil lost its fertility.

But that is not the complete story. For even in ancient times, the irrigation systems faced difficulties. Silt brought down from the mountains by the great rivers was slowly deposited in the river beds and irrigation canals, clogging them and changing their courses. At the same time, salts from the river water were continually being added to the soil. These salts decreased the yield, especially for certain crops, such as wheat. For this reason, there was a gradual shift over the centuries from wheat to barley as a food crop. But even for barley, the yield was continually shrinking, with the result that starvation faced greater and greater numbers of people. There is no question, therefore, in the minds of many scientists, that the increase of salt and silt played an important role in the destruction of Sumerian power. Later, shortly before the beginning of the Christian era, a new irrigation system was constructed, and for many centuries this permitted the peasants to increase their crop yields. But the new system was even more sensitive to destruction than the old, and by 1200 A.D. had become completely useless. Iraq turned into a desert.

The modern government of Iraq, aware of the need for an agricultural revolution, faces the same difficulties the Sumerians faced five thousand years ago. It has therefore decided to profit by Sumerian experience, and has hired teams of archaeologists, geologists, and soil scientists to make an archaeological survey of the changes in river beds, irrigation systems, soil fertility, and so on, over the centuries, in order that the peasants of modern Iraq may be able to grow better crops. In this case the value of archaeology *can* be measured in dollars and cents.

Having noted all this, we must still emphasize that the

chief value of archaeology is quite different. Even before it was applied to the improvement of agriculture, the study of man's material remains did have an extremely important use: it has been and continues to be a science which helps us understand the place of the human species in nature and gives us perspective in viewing humanity as a whole.

Let us consider an analogy. When a physician faces a new patient who presents baffling symptoms, his first step is to take a case history, recording childhood illnesses, accidents, vaccinations, diseases to which relatives were prone, deaths of brothers and sisters, and so on. Often the history alone is enough to reveal the patient's ailment.

In the same way the archaeologist studies the childhood and adolescence of *his* subject, the human race, with all its early episodes of disaster and achievement, not with the intention of prescribing treatment, but with the hope, perhaps, of learning the race's weaknesses and strength. As he goes further back into the past, he finds no Paleolithic records of chiefs and battles, of victories and defeats. This is all to the good. The very nature of the archaeological record over the centuries has forced him to become interested in the genuinely significant events of that distant era.

These events include the realization that fire could be man's friend as well as his foe. They include small and seemingly trifling discoveries such as the manner of chipping flints, of fitting the flints into bone or wooden handles, and of using the implements thus obtained. They include the sudden realization that a study of the heavens could help guide a sailor across a sea or a herdsman across a trackless waste, or could tell a farmer the best time to plant his crop. They embrace even such simple inspirations as using the fingers of both hands instead of one to count on.

For too many centuries, historians were concerned chiefly with the names of kings and the dates of battles. It is only within the past hundred years or so that attention has shifted from rulers to the people they ruled, and in this change of emphasis archaeology has played a large role.

It has served other functions as well. Obscure passages in the Bible as well as in Homer take on new meaning as we become aware of the conditions under which their authors lived and wrote. In addition, excavation has uncovered and translated entire new literatures. Egyptian plays and Babylonian epics have been added to our stock of cultural treasures. And some of the world's most beautiful art and architecture have been bequeathed us by the cave dwellers of Altamira, the artisans of Egypt and Crete, and the painters and sculptors of Greece.

The history of the theatre, poetry, art, architecture, mathematics, astronomy, chemistry, and other branches of science, as well as of the human race itself would be incomplete and often recorded erroneously if not for the contributions of archaeology. And the history of any subject is a part of it.

Neither nations nor the human race as a whole live by bread alone. Nations live by pride in the achievements of their ancestors, the memory of past glories sustaining them through periods of difficulty and giving hope for the future. For centuries a divided and conquered Italy nourished its dreams with memories of Rome, just as the modern Greeks recalled their own land's ancient splendor. In countries of Asia and Africa long subject to foreign rule, the discovery of greatness in the past has meant a determination to attain greatness again in the future.

That is why such different governments as those of Italy, Greece, Turkey, Egypt, and China support archaeological research. Not one of these is a wealthy country, and one might say that money spent on digging ruins might better be devoted to growing more food, or to improving the social structure. But without a spirit of hope for the future there can be neither food nor social improvement.

Historical and archaeological studies let a people know what its powers can be. Sometimes these studies are misused by governments which exaggerate the achievements of the past at the expense of national rivals. Like other sciences, archaeology can be exploited for evil ends. But it has a proper function in showing us that great achievements are limited to no nation, no race, no geographic area. In some of the most unlikely areas in the world, the one thing necessary to uncover evidence of a great past has been to dig properly. At different times in history, different nations and races have forged to the front intellectually or politically. In every case supremacy has been only temporary, and no matter how high a country has risen it has depended on the accomplishments of its predecessors and its neighbors. The Sumerians learned from the people who came before them, the Egyptians and Babylonians inherited from the Sumerians, the Greeks started on the basis of what Egyptians and Babylonians had achieved. In the New World, Aztecs and Incas borrowed from the other tribes of Mexico and Peru.

These facts can of course be interpreted from the pessimists' point of view. Does not the rise and fall of civilizations, they point out, indicate the futility of human effort? All countries, whether they remain great powers for centuries or for mere decades, face the same eventual fate: a fall from the heights, often complete disaster. You cannot, say the pessimists, change human destiny. And to this they add, "You can't change human nature. It has been the same through the ages and will remain the same."

Archaeology does not pretend to give the answer to this question. But it does furnish evidence from which you can make up your own mind about the answer.

In many ways we feel close kinship to men and women who lived long ago. When we read the story of Joseph and his brethren in the Bible, we share the emotions of Joseph when he is torn from his home, tempted by Potiphar's wife, thrown into prison, and finally, having risen to greatness, encounters his brothers again, not in a spirit of revenge, but with love and forgiveness. The cave paintings of Altamira were created many thousands of years earlier, and we can share the feeling of beauty that inspired the artist. What more evidence is needed that human nature has not changed?

Let us go still further back—say, two million years. At this time there was no such thing as human nature because there were no human beings. There was only ape nature, which in the course of time became human. And yet if we observe apes in a zoo (and chimpanzees and gorillas are both more primitive than our ancestors of 2,000,000 B.C.) or the still less human monkeys, we can still see traits like our own, from curiosity and the desire to show off before visitors, to affection for a favorite, whether fellow ape or human keeper. Similarities exist between us and other, less related mammals, as well. Anyone who has ever owned a dog will recognize in how many respects dogs resemble children.

But in many ways dogs differ from children, as we differ from apes and from the human beings of twenty thousand or two thousand or for that matter of two hundred years ago. True, we are of a different species from the apes, while there is no evidence of biological difference between us and the men of 18,000 B.C. But close similarity in a number of traits does not imply identity of nature. We may not be better or worse. We *are* different.

It is usually when we recall the viler aspects of human nature that we have our doubts. Wars still exist, and cruelty to fellow human beings. The mass slaughter of their enemies by the ancient Assyrians is more than matched by the slaughter carried out by modern Nazis. On our side as well as the enemy's, soldiers, from privates to commanders-in-chief, acquire a lust for killing, and persuade themselves that they kill, no matter what the circumstances, for patriotic reasons only.

And yet there have been changes. Archaeologists frown at the idea that it is "human nature" that has changed. To them the word seems difficult to define, and therefore unscientific. They prefer to talk of *cultures,* which are in the first place assemblages of types found at a number of sites, and in the second, the patterns of behavior characteristic of the people who created those types. But by "human nature" most of us mean nothing more than the way we think and feel and act, and this is not so different from the archaeologist's "culture."

Cultures have certainly changed tremendously. When we look up at the sky at night, for example, we see a universe of stars and galaxies many light years away. To us the sun is a mass of hot gas engaged in nuclear reactions, and the moon a cold satellite. To primitive men, Sun and Moon were gods. To us mountains and seas are part of inanimate Nature, products of several billion years of evolution. To primitive men they were the abodes of gods and demons.

In many respects the experiences of one group of men inevitably differ from those of another, and hence their thinking and feeling, their "culture," their "human nature" do as well. Biologically, human beings have changed little for thousands of years, but far from being constant from one millennium to the next, human nature changes at least every generation and indeed is different from one man to the next.

Archaeology offers us the evidence of what man's nature was in the past, as its related science of ethnology does for the present. It shows us what we were, and lets us judge for ourselves what we may become. If it did nothing but this, it would more than justify its right to exist. It may never make us richer, but it will certainly make us wiser, and more capable of judging whether riches are the goals we should seek in life.

GLOSSARY

ANTHROPOLOGY : a historical and functional study of mankind throughout the world in terms of culture, language, and biology. The divisions are: ethnology, archaeology, linguistics, and physical anthropology.

ARAMAIC : a group of Semitic languages, including the language used by Christ.

ARCHAEOLOGY : the scientific study of ancient man by means of investigating his material remains and environment.

ARTIFACT : an object, or alteration in a natural object, produced by human workmanship.

ARYAN : the original Indo-European language; often applied inaccurately to all primitive people who spoke this language, specifically and accurately to the Causasoid invaders of India.

BACTERIOLOGY : the science of bacteria, or tiny organisms.

BOTANY : the science of plants and plant life.

BRONZE AGE : a stage in human culture in which tools were made of an alloy of copper and tin; presumably begun in 3000 B.C. in Egypt and Asia Minor, much later in other parts of the world.

CAMERA LUCIDA : a device which projects the image of an object on paper to permit tracing of its outline.

CARBON-14: a radioactive form of carbon produced by the action of cosmic rays on nitrogen of the air.

CARBON-14 DATING: a method for dating ancient objects by determining the radioactivity due to carbon-14. (Also called radiocarbon dating.)

CHALCOLITHIC : related to the early part of the Bronze Age, in which the transition was made from the use of stone to that of bronze by using copper.

CRO-MAGNON MAN : a prehistoric race named for the Cro-Magnon cave, where its remains were first found; considered to be of the same species as modern man.

CRYPTOGRAPHY : the study of cipher writing and secret characters.

CULTURE : traits manifested by a tribe or group of men which unite the group in a pattern of living; in archaeology, a large collection of types of pottery, weapons, tools, etc.

CUNEIFORM : the form of writing used by the Sumerians and other ancient peoples; produced by the impressions of square-edged tools on clay.

DEMOTIC SCRIPT : the simplified, popular form which arose out of ancient Egyptian writing.

DENDROCHRONOLOGY : the determination of dates by counting tree rings.

DYNASTY : a succession of rulers supposedly descended from the same line or family.

GLOSSARY

EGYPTOLOGY : the study of ancient Egypt.

EOLITHIC AGE : the earliest stage of human culture, in which the tools used were so crude as to make it uncertain that they were tools at all.

ETHNOBOTANY : the study of those plants of importance to people.

ETHNOLOGY : a division of anthropology concerned with the comparative study of cultures throughout the world.

FLAKED STONES : stones from which pieces were flaked off by striking with other stones.

FLINT : a hard stone used by primitive man for tools and weapons; a tool or weapon made from such stone.

FOSSIL : the remains of plant or animal life from a previous geological period, preserved in rock formations.

GEOLOGY : the science of the earth as a whole and of its rocks and fossils, its rivers, its oceans, etc.

HIERATIC SCRIPT : a form of hieroglyphic writing.

HIEROGLYPHICS : pictures or symbols representing words, syllables, or sounds used by the ancient Egyptians; the system of writing using such pictures or symbols.

HOMO : Man; the genus of advanced apes composed of modern man and several of his extinct predecessors.

HOMO NEANDERTHALENIS : Neanderthal Man, named for the Neander Valley where his bones were first discovered.

GLOSSARY

Homo Sapiens: "Wise Man," or our present human species.

Indo-European : the family of languages now spoken in large parts of Europe and Southwest Asia, India, etc., presumably derived from a single ancient language.

Iron Age : a period of civilization in which iron implements and weapons were used; the Age which followed the Bronze Age in much of the Old World (or Europe and Asia).

Kitchen Midden : a mound of kitchen leavings, composed of animal bones, shells, and other refuse marking the site of a prehistoric settlement.

Lake Dwelling : a prehistoric dwelling built on wooden piles rising (originally) above the surface of a lake.

Linear A : a script or system of writing of ancient Crete, based on Akkadian, the language of the Babylonians.

Linear B : a script derived from Linear A, adapted to the Greek language.

Linguistics : the study of human speech, including the origin, structure, and modification of languages.

Mesolithic Age : the Middle Stone Age, a transitional age between the use of primitive and more advanced stone implements and weapons.

Neolithic Age : the New Stone Age, when highly developed stone tools were used; the age preceding the Bronze Age.

Oceanography : the study of the oceans, their geology, their chemistry, their animal life, etc.

PALEO- : a prefix meaning ancient; thus paleobiology, paleobotany, paleochemistry, etc., are the study of the life, the plants, the chemistry, etc., of the ancient world.

PALEOLITHIC AGE : the Old Stone Age, when the tools made were still relatively crude, but none the less recognizable as tools.

PAPYRUS : a writing material made from reeds which grew in the Nile and other rivers; used by ancient Egyptians, Greeks, and Romans for manuscripts and important documents.

PHYSICAL ANTHROPOLOGY : the study of human evolution and the present races of man, a division of anthropology.

SILT : fine-grained soil and sand deposited by water.

STRATA : in geology and archaeology, layers of earth and rock, distinguishable by color, texture, etc.

TYPE : a characteristic artifact found at a site of ancient habitation.

TYPOLOGY : a system of classification of artifacts by types, used as an aid to the dating of cultures.

VARVE : a layer of sedimentary material, usually deposited in a lake by water from a melting glacier in a single year; used to date ancient deposits.

VOLCANOLOGY: the study of volcanoes.

ZOOLOGY : the science of animal life.

BIBLIOGRAPHY

ALBRIGHT, W. F., *Archaeology and the Religion of Israel*, Johns Hopkins, Baltimore, 1952.

BAIKIE, JAMES, *Egyptian Antiquities of the Nile Valley*, Macmillan, New York, 1932.

BLEGEN, CARL W., ed., *Troy*, Princeton University Press, Princeton, 1952.

CHILDE, V. GORDON, *The Dawn of European Civilization*, Routledge and Kegan Paul, London, 1952.

Man Makes Himself, Watts, London, 1951.

New Light on the Most Ancient East, Routledge and Kegan Paul, London, 1952.

Piecing Together the Past, F. A. Praeger, New York, 1956.

What Happened in History, Penguin, London, 1942.

CLARK, J. G. D., *Prehistoric Europe*, Methuen, London, 1952.

DANIEL, G. E., *A Hundred Years of Archaeology*, Duckworth, London, 1950.

DIRINGER, D., *The Alphabet*, Hutchinson, London, 1949.

EVANS, SIR ARTHUR J., *The Palace of Minos*, Macmillan, London, 1935.

EDWARDS, I. E. S., *The Pyramids of Egypt*, Penguin, London, 1947.

FRANKFURT, H., *The Birth of Civilization in the Near East*, Doubleday, New York, 1956.

FRANKFURT, E. and H. A., WILSON, J. A., and JACOBSEN, T., *Before Philosophy*, Penguin, London, 1949.

HEIZER, R. F., *Manual of Archaeological Field Methods*, The National Press, Palo Alto, California, 1950.

HEYERDAHL, THOR, *Aku-Aku, The Secret of Easter Island*, Rand McNally, Chicago, 1958.

[216]

BIBLIOGRAPHY

KENYON, F., *The Bible and Archaeology*, Harper, New York, 1940.

KENYON, K. M., *Beginnings in Archaeology*, Praeger, New York, 1953.

KRAMER, S. N., *From the Tablets of Sumer*, Falcon's Wing Press, New York, 1956.

MACKAY, E. J. H., *Early Indus Civilizations*, Luzac, London, 1948.

MORLEY, S. G., *The Ancient Maya*, Stanford University Press, Stanford, California, 1947.

OAKLEY, K. P., *Man the Tool Maker*, British Museum of Natural History, London, 1950.

PENDLEBURY, J. S., *Tell el Amarna*, Lovat Dickson and Thompson, London, 1935.

The Archaeology of Crete, Methuen, London, 1939.

SINGER, C., HOLMYARD, E. J., and HALL, A. R., *A History of Technology*, Oxford University Press, New York, 1954.

VAILLANT, G. C., *The Aztecs of Mexico*, Penguin, London, 1950.

VON HAGEN, V. W., *The Realm of the Incas*, New American Library, New York, 1957.

WACE, A. J. B., *Mycenae*, Princeton U. Press, Princeton, 1949.

WHEELER, SIR M., *Archaeology from the Earth*, Clarendon Press, Oxford, 1954.

WOOLLEY, SIR C. L., *Digging Up the Past*, Crowell, New York, 1954.

Ur of the Chaldees, Penguin, London, 1940.

Some of the above listed books are published, by different publishers, in other editions than those cited. News of archaeology appears in *American Antiquity, Antiquity,* and *Archaeology.* Reports on the relations of archaeology and the different sciences can be found in *Science* and *Nature.*

INDEX

INDEX

INDEX

INDEX

[224]